FRONT GARDENS

FRONT GARDENS

GAY SEARCH

BBC BOOKS

ACKNOWLEDGEMENTS

We would like to thank the following people and companies who helped greatly in the creation of the gardens featured in *Front Gardens*:

John Massey (Ashwood Nurseries) West Midlands; Marshalls, Halifax; Worcester Nurseries, Worcester; Robin Tacchi Nurseries; Town and Country Paving Ltd, West Sussex; Kennedy's Garden Centre, Berks; Borderstone – Border Hardcore and Rockery Stone Co Ltd, Powys; Renzland Forge Ltd, Essex; Smiths Concrete Ltd, Oxon: Coleford Brick and Tile Co Ltd, Gloucs; Redland Aggregates, Leics; Ready Mixed Concrete (UK) Ltd, Middx; Hozelock Ltd, Bucks; Leaky Pipe Garden Systems, Suffolk; Lotus Water Products, Lancs; Wythall Roofing Centre Ltd, Solihull; Wythall Tool Hire, Birmingham; Vincent Timber Ltd, Birmingham; Butterleys Brick Ltd, Derby; Freshfield Lane Bricks, East Sussex; Agriframes, West Sussex; Haddonstone, Northampton; Hardy Fencing, Gloucs; Woodlodge, Surrey; Do It All Ltd, West Midlands; Forest Fencing, Nr Worcester; Larchlap, Worcs; Stonemarket, Warwickshire; Solopark, Cambridge; Dennis Ruabon Ltd, Clwyd; Sussex Herbs, Sussex; Olive Tree Terracotta Pots, Hampshire; Whichford Potteries, Warwickshire; Mariner Tool Hire, Staffordshire; Building and Garden Supplies, Sutton Coldfield; ARC Central, Leicestershire; Fiskars UK Ltd, Mid Glamorgan; Wolf Tools, Herefordshire; Spear and Jackson Garden Products, London.

We would also like to thank Michael Twite Landscapes, EDD Training Services and the Parks Department, City of Birmingham, and Soltrain of Solihull College.

For full details of the products used and suppliers' addresses, please send a large (A4) SAE to: Catalyst Television, Brook Green Studios, 186 Shepherds Bush Road, London W6 7LL

Published by BBC Books,
a division of BBC Enterprises Limited,
Woodlands, 80 Wood Lane, London W12 0TT
First published 1993
© Gay Search 1993

ISBN 0 563 36713 X

All photographs by Marianne Majerus except those on pages 24 (*top*), 87 (*top*), 130 (*top*), and 138 (*top*) by Stephen Hamilton

Set in 11/13 Plantin Light by Goodfellow & Egan Ltd., Cambridge
Printed and bound in Great Britain by Butler & Tanner Ltd., Frome, Somerset
Colour separations by Technik Ltd, Berkhamsted
Jacket printed by Belmont Press Ltd, Northampton

CONTENTS

CHAPTER ONE

*I*NTRODUCTION

M ost gardeners find it much more difficult to create an attractive garden at the front of their house than they do at the back. You only have to drive through any city, town or suburb in this country to realise that the front gardens that really catch your eye are few and far between, while the rest are at best, uninspiring, and at worst, badly neglected.

It would seem that many people who take pride and pleasure in their *back* gardens just don't know where to start when it comes to the front.

One explanation could be that front gardens are public, on display to everyone passing by, and that, for a race as reserved as we British, is a large part of the problem. As Alfred Austin, one of the lesser known Victorian Poets Laureate and a keen gardener, once wrote, 'Show me your garden, provided it be your own, and I will tell you what you are like!'

Perhaps that's what we're afraid of, for there's no doubt that the front garden offers our visitors the first clue about us. Perhaps the reason that so many front gardens are so dull is that we would rather do the bare minimum and be thought unimaginative than try something a little different and be thought pretentious, or worse still, lacking in taste!

To be fair, there are also a number of other practical factors that make front gardens much more of a challenge. For a start, they have a totally different function to back gardens. A back garden is for leisure and relaxation, whether that's actually gardening or just sitting in a deck chair. A front garden has to fulfil a number of different roles, which means you have to work within a number of different, tightly drawn parameters.

First of all, the front garden separates your home from the street. We humans are territorial animals and the front garden is a physical buffer against traffic noise and pollution, against other people's children, dogs and litter. Equally important, it's also a psychological buffer, whether the actual barrier is a six foot high hedge or just a single strand of spiked plastic chain, looped between short posts.

At the same time, the front garden is also our link to the outside world and one of its primary functions is allowing access to and from the house. Necessity dictates that there has to be a path between the street and the front door that will stand up to lots of wear and tear, and which will allow relatively clean, dry access. You can get away with mown lawn paths or stepping stones in the back garden, but they are just not suitable at the front.

In theory, you could site the front gate and the path anywhere you like, but if it's not in the most logical position, which is usually the shortest route from A to B, you'll find the milkman and the postman will beat their own path to your door – straight across the lawn or through your flowerbeds. Landscape designers call these routes 'desire lines', which makes them sound a lot more interesting than the reality – the postman's size nines right through the middle of your aubrieta! One particularly successful small town front garden did, in fact, put in a double dog-leg path from the gate to the front door, to create an illusion of greater space, but discouraged anyone from taking the logical short cut by planting a very large spiky mahonia at the critical point where the path bends!

Then, unglamorous as they are, there are the dustbins to think about. If you live in a terraced house, then for functional reasons they have to be put at the front, where they do nothing at all for the look of your garden.

Your choice of plants and where you put them should take into account the passing pedestrian traffic, too. As a general rule, plants in front gardens need to be tougher than those you'd choose for the back. Some delicate little treasure planted on the corner of a bed is unlikely to escape the dustman's boots for long! But you can make this work to your advantage: some plants only give off their perfume when the leaves and stems are crushed, so what better to line the garden path with than, say, lavender or thyme? One gardener I know has a huge, bushy rosemary growing by his front door. Nearly all his visitors pick a sprig to sniff while they're waiting to be let in – the main reason, he believes, that his rosemary is so bushy!

While it's quite possible not to set foot in your back garden all winter, you will be walking through your front garden practically every day of the year, and so you'll want something that looks as good as possible all year round. That means including a good proportion of evergreens in your plant selection – between a third and a half, probably – though do remember that 'evergreens' needn't be *green*. You need only think of wonderful golden variegated shrubs like *Eleagnus pungens* 'Maculata'; the plain gold shrubby honeysuckle (*Lonicera nitida* 'Baggesen's Gold'), the creams and greens of *Euonymus fortunei* 'Emerald Gaiety' or the silvers of *Artemisia* and cotton lavender (*Santolina*) to realise that a garden with a large proportion of evergreens can be colourful all year round. Incidentally, plain greens have their place, too, to set off the more colourful foliage, and it's worth remembering that shiny green foliage on plants like *Fatsia japonica*, and the Mexican orange blossom (*Choisya ternata*) will reflect light, making it look brighter and more interesting than matt green foliage which absorbs light.

Think about scent, too. What could be nicer on a bright, cold morning than the fragrance of winter-flowering viburnum, or be more welcoming as you open the front gate on a summer's evening than the sweet perfume of jasmine, lilies or tobacco plants?

These days, it's not just people who need access to your house. Until we all go Green and get on our bikes, the car will continue to loom large in many front gardens. With street parking becoming more and more difficult in towns and cities, and unless you have a garage, you'll need some kind of hardstanding for a car or, increasingly commonly, cars. In any urban area you'll see the worst examples of how this problem has been tackled: terraced house gardens completely concreted over and suburban semis fronted by a vast expanse of tarmac – with possibly a tree or a couple of shrubs parked in a corner as reminders that front gardens used to be places where people grew plants.

There are practical considerations to be borne in mind. You'll need a driveway wide enough for passengers to get out of the car without ending up in the flowerbeds, which takes a large chunk out of the average-sized front garden but by combining the path and driveway you'll be taking one chunk, not two.

However you design the hard landscaping necessary for a car, though, it will be all too easy for it to dominate, so it's very important that the planting is able to compete. By using some strong vertical lines – small trees, large shrubs and so on – you will balance the strong horizontal lines of the hard surfaces. Beds or borders of low-growing plants won't do a great deal to minimise the impact of the paving or tarmac.

Another important function of the front garden is to provide the setting for the house itself, so relating it to the architecture is more important here than it is at the back. Remember that you look at your front garden with the house as the backdrop most of the time, so house and garden should complement each other.

When you're planning your front garden, you need at least to consider the architectural style of your house, whether it's a country cottage, a Victorian family house, a between-the-wars semi, 1950s council house, or a modern estate townhouse. That's not to say that your garden has to be a museum piece, and that you have to reproduce the kind of garden that went with the house when it was originally built. But it does mean that a picket fence, and cottage style garden will look much better fronting a country cottage than, say, a Victorian house or a 1930s semi.

If you do live in an old house, you may well be within a conservation area, and so plans will have to conform to certain regulations. You may find that trees and hedges are protected by conservation orders and you touch them, without permission from the planning authority, at your peril! It may also be that the type of walls, fences, railings

This small front garden is both in sympathy and, just as important, in scale
with the nineteenth-century terraced cottage behind it. The formal beds
round the edge, separated by gravel paths from the diamond-shaped central
bed, all filled with colourful bedding, are very Victorian in style.

and gates you can put up are also subject to regulations, so always check with the town hall first. The plus is that if you *do* live in a conservation area and it's one that has been made a priority by English Heritage (tel: 071 973 3000) they may well give you a grant towards the cost of repairing or reinstating the original gate and railings.

While you can erect walls and fences up to 2 m (6 ft 6 in) in your *back* garden with impunity, any wall or fence that 'abuts the public highway' and is higher than 1 m (3 ft 3 in) needs planning permission. The slightly daft thing is that in most places you can plant a *Leylandii* hedge in the front garden and let it grow as high as you like!

If you live in a Garden City like Welwyn, Letchworth, or Bourneville you will probably find that restrictive covenants cover the public areas of your home – the front garden and the front of the house – which means you must seek permission before you remove trees, uproot hedges, build or demolish walls, or even lay new hardstanding for cars. Welwyn Garden City, for example, takes the view that front gardens are a very important part of the communal landscaping, and that if you were to take out all the hedges and trees you would be left with an unattractive, harsh, urban environment. To make sure this doesn't happen, written permission is necessary before cutting, lopping or topping trees that are over 15 ft in height, removing boundary hedges or replacing front lawns and flower beds with crazy paving.

Other local authorities have their rules, too, although how strictly these are enforced varies from place to place. One of the front gardens in the series was in an open plan area where no barriers over 75 cm (30 in) – whether walls, fences or hedges – were allowed without permission and transgressors were made to remove anything over that limit.

It is also common for new housing developments to have restrictive covenants which could stop you putting up hedges or fences in the front garden at least for, say, three or five years. So if a quick glance around your estate doesn't reveal any visible boundaries, check with the developers before you go ahead.

Some council estates also enforce restrictions, although few local authorities today are likely to be as cavalier as the Shrewsbury Housing Committee in the 1950s, when it issued an order to tenants 'to clear their front gardens of any kind of fences, kerbs and ornaments they have built'. One commentator at the time praised the Committee for 'having recognised vulgarity in the gardens on the estate and for condemning it.'

When it comes to design, modern houses are more of a challenge because there is as yet no tradition to follow. But that doesn't mean that any old style from the past, chosen at random, can be imposed on them. Again, the traditional cottage garden with a picket fence or a formal Victorian garden with carpet bedding just wouldn't look right. However, there is no reason why elements from different styles can't be adapted to a new environment and married together successfully.

Insofar as you can lay down overall design guidelines for front gardens, the most important for any style of house would be, keep it simple. Most front gardens are rather small and since the space between the street and your house is already divided up by paths and driveways, chopping it up even further with lots of beds will make it look smaller still. And cutting beds out of a lawn will also make maintenance a bit of a nightmare.

Perhaps we are wedded to our bit of lawn in the front, even if it is mossy, patchy and weed-ridden and, in the case of a terraced property, does involve lugging the mower through the house once a week, because the only alternative we can think of is the dreaded tarmac or paving. But of course the right type of paving can be very attractive and in a very small garden, the best solution may be to combine hard landscaping, using paving, bricks or gravel with soft planting.

When it comes to choosing the colour of the plants for your front garden, especially close to the house, either in a border or in hanging baskets and window boxes, it's important to consider the colours of the house itself. Red or deep blue flowers tend to disappear rather against red brick, while acid yellows and orange could clash violently. Paler colours, on the other hand, stand out. However, against a white wall, bright reds, deep blues and acid yellows look more striking than pale colours and in some cases, using just one strong colour theme can look even better. One white house had troughs, wall pots and hanging baskets filled with bright yellow wallflowers adorning its wrought iron balcony, and the effect was absolutely stunning.

Take a good look at your paintwork. Wouldn't it look better if it was all the same colour rather than several different ones? You could always spray-paint existing window boxes to match and paint your fence the same colour as your front door and window frames.

Look at the house as a backdrop to your garden and think about how you can relate the two to get the best out of both. If the fabric of the house is basically unexciting – garish modern brick or cement-coloured render, for example – imagine how much better it would look with climbers like Virginia creeper, ivy, roses or Clematis growing up it, or evergreen wall shrubs such as firethorn (*Pyracantha*) or Cotoneaster trained against it. The owners of one London house with a large bay window also did away with the need for net curtains by planting Cotoneaster beneath the window, growing to about 25 cm (10 in) above the bottom of the glass. They looked out through windows framed by open arched branches of Cotoneaster and passers-by couldn't see inside.

If you're a really keen gardener then of course a front garden is yet more space in which to practise your hobby. What makes it interesting is that it will be the opposite aspect from the back garden. If it's north facing, say, it will provide you with the perfect conditions to grow shade-loving plants. It's also an opportunity for you to create a garden that's completely different in style and mood. If your back garden is romantic and informal, for instance, you could design a front garden with a more classical feel.

Finally of course, to come full circle, an attractive front garden will add to the amenity of the neighbourhood and the pleasure of passers by. Think how your own spirits are lifted by a pretty front garden that you pass every day. To an extent, you need to consider your neighbours and the other gardens around you when planning your own. Unless you're very brave – or a bit eccentric – you won't want your garden to stick out like a sore thumb. That doesn't mean you must slavishly copy what everyone else has (or all too often, hasn't!) done, but it does mean you should think twice before creating a scale model of the Matterhorn or a topiary version of Concorde!

It also means thinking very carefully about what trees, shrubs and hedges to plant and where to site them. Many a neighbourly relationship has been ruined by the gigantic *Leylandii* hedge which casts deep shade and sucks all the goodness out of the soil on both sides, or the weeping willow that undermines friendships as well as foundations.

On new estates where formal front boundaries are banned, one solution would be to co-operate with your neighbours in planting areas of trees and shrubs.

Another factor that, sadly, has to be borne in mind is green-fingered crime. We've always had to tolerate the impulsive child picking daffodils but these days it's tubs, window-boxes and hanging baskets that go walking – thefts that involve some degree of planning since you don't simply take away a large tub full of heavy damp soil and a standard bay tree, on impulse. You can only try to make the movables less movable, by wiring hanging baskets to their brackets, for instance, cementing pots and ornaments in place or making them heavier with a good layer of ballast in the bottom – anything that will make it more difficult for a thief to remove them.

As for the real front gardens whose transformations are featured in the book and the series which it accompanies, we asked six top garden designers to solve the common problems each one had and to create gardens that the owners could manage and enjoy. I hope you will find inspiration here for your own front plot, but if yours has different problems that you can't solve yourself, it could be well worth calling in a professional garden designer, whose objective and experienced eye will probably come up with a solution you'd never have thought of! A design and a planting plan needn't cost that much, and indeed could save you money in the long run. What *is* expensive is getting a garden built, but don't forget, once you have a master plan, you can tackle various areas as you can afford to, and you can keep the costs down considerably, as we did, by doing some, if not all the work yourself. If you are competent at DIY, then there's no reason why you can't lay drives or even build walls yourself. If you're not so skilled, then do the labouring and pay a craftsman – a brickie, say – to do the more difficult tasks.

But however you set about it, creating a beautiful front garden, which you, your family and the neighbours can enjoy, will give you enormous satisfaction and pleasure every day for years to come.

CHAPTER TWO

THE VICTORIAN GARDEN

*T*he Victorian era is of particular interest because that's when the front garden as we know it today really came into being. Before then, houses were owned either by the very rich, whose acres of parkland or ornate *parterres* in the style of Versailles were tended by armies of gardeners or, at the other end of the scale, by cottagers whose small patches of garden were farmed in order to feed their families.

What made the Victorian age so different was the rise of the home-owning middle classes, who lived in the substantial villas, semis and terraced houses of the suburbs, each with its own front garden, many of which are still standing and in which many of us live today. It was also a time of growing prosperity, where people were not ashamed of having 'got on', and so the front gardens of their new homes were the place to display their newly achieved wealth and taste.

So the Victorian front garden was very much designed to be seen from the street. According to a book published in 1855 by leading Victorian garden writer, Shirley Hibbard, entitled *The Town Garden*, front plots '. . . if well kept, add very much to the neatness, cheerfulness and indeed respectability of a house. Just as we may judge a man by his dress and general bearing, so we may judge him by the appearance of his home.'

Mr Hibbard had clear advice for the Victorian front gardener: 'Lay out the plot in the simplest manner possible and do not suffer your neighbours to laugh at an endless variety of *parterres* of all shapes and sizes, edged with oyster shells and filled up with plants that would disgrace a common. One central bed and a continuous border are usually all you have room for, or at least three (always prefer odd numbers) beds of equal sizes, and in these you may keep up a show of annuals and herbaceous perennials. The centre of each bed should have a handsome flowering shrub and near the house one or two laurels and a holly will serve as a screen against dust and ensure privacy for your windows . . . A very small plot is best laid down with grass or clean gravel, without flowers at all. In the centre a variegated holly, box tree or laurel may be planted; and all the labour required is to keep the grass close shaven or the gravel neatly swept. Here the object must be to produce a neat appearance and to avoid all attempts at bewildering outlines, massive shrubbery or thin sprinklings of innumerable colours.'

Four years on, it was obvious that in general the Victorian gardener had not followed Mr Hibbard's advice, as he laments in the revised edition of his book: 'You will see in front of fine establishments pyramids of brick planted with ferns and trailing plants, piles of stone and wild masses of shrub, even rustic arbours with thatched roofs and sometimes a few garden seats. I see plenty such in my walks about the suburbs, and I sigh for the abolition of tea houses where such notions seem to have been picked up.'

However, by the middle of the decade, the dominant style of both semis and terraces was what the garden historian Sir Roy Strong calls 'the geometric gardenesque'. This often meant a tessellated path leading straight from the front gate to the front door, usually on the far right or far left of the house and often in black-and-white or red-and-black tiling, with glazed terracotta rope twist tiles between the path and the very narrow border on one side and the rest of the garden on the other.

The main section of the garden often contained a formal geometric pattern of beds surrounded by gravel or grass. Cutting the grass in such a garden was even more difficult than it is today, when we have the advantage of lightweight powered machinery, but a real status symbol in Victorian suburbia was a new grass-cutting machine – and that small patch of lawn told passers-by that this particular householder was rich enough to afford one!

There was altogether a great deal in the mid-Victorian front garden that had more to do with status than with horticulture. A then rare tree – like the Monkey puzzle – a sundial or a large urn were all displays of the householder's wealth. As for planting, the Victorians had a passion for bedding, shared today only by a few parks departments with enough money to afford it. Block bedding (using masses of plants all in the same colour to form geometric patterns) and ribbon bedding (planting in stripes of colour) were both popular, but the big attraction was for carpet bedding – making intricate patterns out of hundreds of different bedding plants.

This type of planting also confirmed status. The nursery trade, which grew all these plants, was just getting into full swing, and a garden full of showy bedding, set out in late May or June and discarded with the first frosts in autumn, indicated that the owner was wealthy enough to afford it.

The Victorians' love of bright, stained-glass colours – reds, golds, purples, oranges – was also reflected in their planting. They also liked exotic plants and, later on in the century, sub-tropical exotics like canna, cordyline and daturas (Angel's Trumpets) were in vogue, grown for the architectural appearance of their foliage rather than their flowers. You still see them today, used as 'dot' plants in formal public bedding schemes.

Towards the end of the century, both William Robinson and Gertrude Jekyll influenced the trend away from formal Victorian planting towards something altogether softer and more informal. Shrub roses instead of standards, and the herbaceous perennials and shrubs started to appear, although the formal bedding schemes lingered on in some gardens well into the twentieth century.

Pollution was the other key factor in the choice of plants, particularly in the Victorian city or town front garden. 'The problem is, how to grow flowers in a soil of cinders and an atmosphere of smoke' explained Shirley Hibbard. That's why plants like privet, laurus-tinus (*Viburnum tinus*) and spotted laurel (*Aucuba japonica*) which can tolerate practically anything, including neglect, became so popular. One of the few pluses in gardening in such conditions was that roses in a Victorian city front garden did not suffer from blackspot – the high concentration of sulphur in the air would have made sure of that.

Towards the end of the nineteenth century, attitudes to front gardens had changed. S. Stackhouse, author of *Hardy Plants for Little Front Gardens*, published around 1890, shared Shirley Hibbard's loathing of rockeries: 'Of all the vulgarities in gardening, none exceeds the vulgarity of an ugly rockery'. In common with many designers today, he preferred a central space of clean dry gravel to the little patch of lawn, and promoted the virtues of an all-year-round garden: 'My ideal front garden has, in the deadest days of winter, a neat, comfortable cared-for appearance.'

If you live in a Victorian house, you may like the idea of a front garden that's perfectly in keeping with it. That's not to say you have to copy the original design slavishly – a garden after all is for pleasure, a living entity, and is not a museum piece. But at least you know there is a garden style that will work well with the house, to which you can refer and use as a starting point.

First of all, try and find anything that might be left of the original features, such as remains of the path (it could still be there under a modern surface, so if you intend taking that up anyway, do so with care) or some old rope twist tiles buried in the soil. These can be cleaned up and supplemented with some of the good new reproductions around.

Boundaries were usually in the form of a hedge (privet or 'laurustinus'), or a low wall with iron work – such as hooped railings along the top – or just iron railings. Even if the original Victorian hedge has survived this long it probably won't be worth keeping, but any man-made boundary can be repaired and restored.

If there is nothing left of the original features then it's worth looking at old photographs of the period to get an idea of what the gardens might have been like. Again, your garden doesn't have to be an exact copy of the original, but it might help you to put

Although very little in this front garden is Victorian, the fact that the front
gate is painted the same sunny colour as the front door helps marry house
and garden very effectively.

down the 'bones' of the garden. If you want to replace the path, for instance, go for a
tessellated one rather than something more modern. If you can't afford to use quarry
tiles, then try concrete slabs in two colours, using one to make small diamond shaped
cut-outs in the corner of the larger ones. You might not be able to afford iron railings but
a picket fence with narrow uprights, painted black, will give a similar effect. If you
decide on a formal hedge, you would be well advised to avoid privet, especially in a very
small garden: not only does it need a lot of looking after but it is very greedy and will
suck valuable moisture and nutrients out of the soil. Instead, if you want a formal hedge,
go for the shrubby honeysuckle (*Lonicera nitida*) in the best green form 'Yunnan' or the
golden variety 'Baggesen's Gold'. A suitable alternative would be box *Buxus sempervirens*. For low hedges within a garden – for edging a knot garden, say – use the dwarf
box (*B.s.* 'Suffruticosa') which won't grow to much more than 75 cm (2ft 6in).

An informal hedge is a softer option, particularly if you already have a low brick wall.
Potentilla fruticosa makes an attractive flowering hedge, as would an evergreen (deciduous
in colder areas) *Escallonia*, the firethorn (*Pyracantha*) or one of the evergreen cotoneasters,

such as the low-growing *C. microphyllus* of which S. Stackhouse wrote: 'If allowed to grow over a low wall, it will trail so prettily downwards at the other side that the passers-by ought to thank the owner: and it is not easily injured by the most idle boy'.

Once you are ready to choose your plants, remember that Victorian-style bedding plants are high cost and high maintenance. But if you like the formal look, you can achieve it by using lovely coloured foliage plants instead. Silvery cotton lavender (*Santolina*) or Lamb's Lugs (*Stachys lanata*) for example, and the wine-red berberis or bugle, *Ajuga reptans* 'Burgundy Glow', all look good for months on end – and they don't need replacing every year.

Painting just the gate posts the same colour as the front door gives this small
Victorian front garden a sense of unity.

Our Victorian gardens

We chose four very small front gardens, each measuring 4.25 × 3.75m (roughly 14 × 12ft), at the end of a row of terraced workman's cottages built in 1888, facing south-west. There were, in fact, two terraces of eleven houses facing each other across a footpath, with a gate from the road at one end, and a brick wall more than 2m (6ft 6in) tall at the other.

We decided to tackle four adjoining gardens, Nos 8,9,10 and 11, rather than just one, because we wanted to show different approaches to creating an attractive front garden in a very small space, and they are just the kind of pocket-handkerchief-sized plots that many people, not only those with Victorian houses, have to deal with these days.

The houses themselves had been sympathetically restored and their original features kept, but most of the gardens were just oblongs of grass, either cut or left long with a sprinkling of dandelions and nettles to liven them up, divided from the central path and from each other by single low horizontal posts. Underneath the small bay window of each of the houses was a large concrete slab where the cellar had been sealed off.

Cathy Harper at No 11, had already planted a few perennials and encouraged the ivy growing to the left of her front door, and along the wall across the end of the street. She is a graphic designer, and had some clear ideas about the kind of garden she wanted. It would be rather formal in its 'bones' – some kind of pattern using bricks or slabs so that she would have a garden to walk through – but less so in its planting. She wanted something that would look good all year round, and the idea of fragrant plants welcoming her home after a hard day's work particularly appealed to her.

Cindy Etheridge at No 10, had put up a low wooden fence round her small plot, initially to stop her dog from running out, but now that she no longer had a dog, she was happy for the fence to go. She had planted a few hybrid tea rose bushes under the windows and hung some garden ornaments on the walls, but what she really wanted was a pretty garden where she could sit out and sunbathe, since the back garden was in shade much of the time.

Richard and Andrew Lynch, two brothers at No 9, readily admitted that they weren't keen gardeners, and so wanted a garden that would look after itself all year round. They liked the idea of a carpet of foliage, in different shades of green, and were keen on the idea of a very small tree. Although they liked the *look* of a small patch of lawn, they admitted they were unlikely to mow it any more regularly than their existing one! They had already decided to repaint their faded red front door forest green, and wanted climbers up the front of the house to soften it a bit.

Tina Rozsas at No 8, had only just moved in and had never had a garden before. She had just started growing indoor house plants and, having found how much she enjoyed that, wanted a garden she could potter in and learn about plants. She wanted climbers around and over the front door – she liked clematis – and wanted flowers in the garden as well as foliage. She was very keen on ivy and her favourite colours were mauve, purple, black and bright red.

The designer of our four Victorian front gardens, Jean Bishop, has worked on many very small gardens, one of which won Gold at Chelsea a few years ago. She has also designed very successful front gardens for small Victorian houses. From archive photographs of similar terraces in the area, it was clear that our houses wouldn't have had gardens as such. There would have been just a communal yard running along the front of all the houses, with a central gully to carry away waste water. The tenants, often families with large numbers of children, would have used the front yard for hanging out washing.

This left Jean free to design four very different gardens, each reflecting some aspect of Victorian style – a tessellated path, for example, a faintly Gothic sunken garden with ferns and ivy, roses climbing through an iron framework – which were not only in sympathy with the houses, but just as important, in scale with them as well. Jean found other ways of giving them a sense of unity, not only with low iron railings around each one, but more subtly by linking each garden with its neighbour. Cathy's garden, for instance, is linked to Cindy's by the use of lavender, teucrium and rosemary on both sides of the boundary, while Cindy's is linked to Richard's by using the same brindle blocks featured on his path for the corner detailing on her paving. The × *Fatshedera* – a cousin of the ivy – on his wall in turn links with the various ivies used in Tina's garden.

For Cathy's garden, Jean solved the problem of creating a garden to walk through in a very small space by making a central paved circle surrounded by circular beds and an outer paved circle, with the path from the entrance and the path to the front door cutting through the beds at an angle. This provided three different routes to the front door, and the narrowness of the paths meant that the herbs would be brushed against, giving off their scent.

Using small granite setts, or a modern substitute, like *Rialta* blocks, was much more in scale with house and garden than the large concrete slabs they replaced, and it meant there were plenty of gaps between them in which plants could self-seed and grow.

By contrast, the planting was very soft and informal, with lots of herbs, and other fragrant plants like Russian sage (*Perovskia atriplicifolia*) to give Cathy the welcome home she wanted, as well as year-round interest. Jean has also created small cobbled half-moon bays around the outer circle to take terracotta pots, so that Cathy can change the displays with the seasons – spring bulbs, for instance, summer bedding and perhaps winter pansies. To take full advantage of the sunny, though currently blank west-facing wall, Jean suggested a fan-trained fruit tree attached to wires fixed along the mortar

The Victorian terrace gardens were pretty unpromising when we started (*left*) but just a few months later, number 11 (*below*) and number 10 (*right*) show very different but equally attractive uses of the same tiny space.

joints. The centrepiece of the garden was a reproduction 'old' terracotta chimney pot filled with attractive variegated ivy.

For Cindy's garden, Jean set out to achieve the decorative look Cindy liked, while at the same time creating not just enough room for sunbathing, but a feeling of space as well. This she achieved very successfully by incorporating the path into the central paved area – done in formal Victorian style using grey paving slabs and brindle blocks as corner decoration. The rose obelisks, made of black plastic-coated steel up which old Victorian favourites like the biscuit-coloured 'Gloire de Dijon' and the rich rose pink 'Reine Victoria' were to grow, gave instant height – always a problem with new gardens – and added to the decorative effect.

The shape of Richard and Andrew's garden was immediately made more interesting by the dog-leg path of herringbone paving blocks. The fact that the front door was on the left of the house and the house was almost always approached from the right, meant that moving the path over to the right, to the centre of the garden, didn't create problems with 'desire lines' – visitors arrived at the new path before the old one! In the centre of the garden Jean created a diamond of green. This would probably have been grass in a Victorian garden but since neither Andrew nor Richard had time to mow it regularly Jean suggested an alternative like thyme, Corsican mint (*Mentha requienii*), which in fact we chose, or even astroturf!

The planting of mainly evergreen foliage shrubs like *Mahonia* 'Charity', *Prunus laurocerasus* 'Otto Luyken', *Euonymus fortunei* and *Viburnum davidii*, with just a few mainly white-flowered plants such as *Lamium* 'White Nancy' and *Bergenia* 'Bressingham White', created the low-maintenance carpet of different greens that Andrew had wanted. Since a covenant prevents owners from planting trees, Jean chose a shrub, *Amelanchier canadensis*, instead, which is open in habit, to allow plants to grow happily in its dappled shade. She chose to site it on the right hand side of the path because what little shade it would cast would suit the plants in Tina's garden better than those in Cindy's.

Red and black are not the easiest of colours to work into a garden but they are among Tina's favourites, and Jean has managed to incorporate them extremely well. The tessellated path, for instance, is a very authentic Victorian checkerboard of red and black quarry tiles, and though Jean has used rope twist tiles here too, she's used them in blue-black rather than terracotta. Alongside lovely red flowering plants like the broom *Cytisus* 'Killiney Red' and *Penstemon* 'Ruby', she has included red foliage plants like the New Zealand flax (*Phormium tenax* 'Dazzler'), as well as the black grass, *Ophiopogon planiscapus* 'Nigrescens'. The sunken middle area in old stone, with a carpet of thyme and ivies around it, gives the garden a wonderful Gothic atmosphere. All four owners were delighted with their gardens, as were the other residents of the terrace, many of whom felt inspired to tackle their own gardens!

VERY SMALL TREES

Most reference books class a 'small tree' as one that grows only to about 35ft! This means that finding a *really* small tree for a small front garden is somewhat of a challenge. The answer is to choose either a very small, very slow growing tree or a slightly larger one with a very light, open habit and delicate leaves, which casts dappled shade. Some of these trees are not widely available, but *The Plant Finder* (£10.99, Moorland Publishing Co Ltd, or try your local library) will tell you which specialist nurseries supply them.

Japanese maple (*Acer palmatum*)
These are among the most beautiful small trees (or shrubs) you can find, and eminently suitable for a Victorian front garden since they were fashionable during that time. They have beautiful, delicate leaves in either bright green, shades of red or purple, or even, in the case of one very recent introduction, *Acer palmatum* 'Ukigumo', variegated green, cream and pink. *Acer palmatum* has hand-shaped leaves, while *A.p.* 'Dissectum' has deeply dissected feathery ones. They form very small, umbrella-shaped trees, which give an attractive outline in winter months. The coral bark maple (*A.p.* 'Senkaki') has lovely red bark in winter as well as good autumn colour and forms a more upright, small tree.

Apart from a lime-free soil, Japanese maples need shelter from cold winds and late spring frosts. They also need protection from strong midday sun which can scorch the foliage very badly, and so a north-facing position or dappled shade is ideal.
Height and spread after 20 years: 2.5 × 2.5 m (8 × 8ft). A.p. 'Senkaki': 4 × 2m (13 × 6ft).

Variegated wedding cake tree (*Cornus controversa* 'Variegata')
This beautiful little tree (or large shrub) gets its common name from the virtually flat layers of foliage separated by lengths of bare stem which resemble the tiers of a wedding cake, and build up slowly over a number of years. The pagoda tree (*C. alternifolia* 'Argentea') is another very similar, slightly smaller-growing variegated tree although the tiers aren't as clearly defined.
Height and spread after 20 years: 5 × 3.5 m (16 × 12ft).

Weeping cotoneaster (*Cotoneaster* × *hybridus pendulus* or *C.* × *watereri pendulus*)
A real 'mini' tree this one, with long trailing stems of semi-evergreen foliage, clusters of small white flowers in early summer and small sealing wax red fruits in winter. If you buy it via mail order make sure you specify you want a weeping standard otherwise you may get a very low-growing ground-cover shrub. Since all weeping cotoneasters are susceptible to fire blight, prevalent in eastern and central England, do check the plant very carefully before you buy.
Height and spread after 20 years: 3 × 4m (10 × 13ft).

The design of the third Victorian terrace garden has a period feel, but would
look equally good in front of a modern town house.

Gleditsia triacanthos 'Elegantissima'
A much smaller-growing relative of the honey locust tree with very delicate light green fern-like foliage which turns yellow in the autumn. Another equally small-growing variety, with slightly weeping branches, is *G.t.* 'Bujotii'. It has bright green foliage which turns an even better golden colour in autumn.
Height and spread after 20 years: 3.5 × 2.5m (12 × 8ft).

Kilmarnock willow (*Salix caprea* 'Pendula')
See page 105.

Kashmir mountain ash (*Sorbus cashmiriana*)
See page 105.

WHEN A SHRUB IS A TREE

Another solution to the problem of very small trees is to grow a shrub as a standard – that is, with its lower branches removed to give you a length of clear stem with the growth on top, like a tree. Bay is often grown this way, but it can also look very effective on a variegated evergreen like *Elaeagnus pungens* 'Maculata' or a holly. You might be able to find standards ready trained in a nursery, or you can do it yourself.

Choose a young shrub with a strong central leading shoot and if it isn't growing straight up, tie it to a cane. When the shrub has reached about 90 cm (3ft) in height, cut back the lowest branches by half their length, and lightly prune the top growths but *excluding* the leader, to encourage bushier growth at the top. The following year, remove the lower laterals completely, cutting them flush with the trunk. (The reason for not cutting them off right away is that they help strengthen and protect the main trunk from damage.) Once the central leader has reached the height you want the *centre* of the head to be, snip it off and lightly prune the remaining growth to make it bushier. If you want something more formal – topiary – then prune it to the shape you want.

PLANTING CONTAINER-GROWN TREES

A tree is – or ought to be – a long term investment for any garden, but it's a salutary fact that more than *half* of all trees and shrubs planted die within the first year, which is not only very discouraging to any gardener but also very expensive.

In a tiny garden, one solitary tree is going to be a star performer, so having chosen an interesting variety to start with you want to make sure it's as healthy as possible and looks as good as it can.

It can't be too strongly stressed that you must never simply dig a hole in uncultivated ground, throw in a bit of organic matter and plant your tree in that. On a clay soil, the hole will act as a sump, drawing water from the land around, so you will be planting your tree in cold, waterlogged soil. If you're lucky, the tree will just be very slow to start into growth. If not, the roots will be deprived of air and will either drown or rot away and the tree will die.

So cultivate all the soil in your border – no great hardship in a very small front garden – before you even think about planting. (See page 124.)

Before you actually start digging your hole, give the tree a thorough soaking while it's still in its container. Not only will it be easier to remove the pot when the time comes, but you are also making sure the roots and the soil around them are really moist before you plant the tree, something that's much more difficult to do once they're in the ground.

Dig a hole slightly bigger than the container. Check that it is deep enough by putting the container in the hole, then laying a bamboo cane or even your spade across it. If the cane rests on the soil both sides *and* the top of the container touches it, then the hole is deep enough.

If your soil is low on organic matter, add a few spadefuls of well-rotted manure or composted straw and a couple of handfuls of fish, blood and bonemeal, or rose fertiliser if you're not an organic gardener, to the pile of soil you've dug out. Then remove the tree carefully from its pot. If it's made of thin black polythene, cut it off with a sharp knife. If the pot is rigid plastic and you've watered it thoroughly beforehand, it should lift out fairly easily. If not, try gently squeezing the sides of the pot just to loosen the soil. If all else fails, you'll have to cut the pot away, using a Stanley knife or something similar.

Place the rootball into the hole and make sure that the tree is facing the right way; many trees have a pretty obvious front if you study their shape. Then start carefully shovelling in the soil. When you've half-filled the hole, firm the soil with the ball of your foot. What you're trying to do is to get rid of any large air pockets in which the roots would dry out and die, without compressing the soil too much, so go gently. Then fill in the hole completely, and firm the soil gently once more.

STAKING

Almost all new trees need staking but recent research has shown that short stakes, reaching only one third of the way up the trunk, are more efficient than the traditional much longer ones. Allowing the top of the tree to sway about in the wind, it seems, thickens the base of the trunk and helps strengthen the root system, so that the tree becomes firmly anchored more quickly.

You'll need a piece of timber 5 × 5 cm (2 × 2 in). To work out the right length, measure the trunk of the tree and divide by three (to give one third its length) and add 45 cm (1 ft 6 in) to hammer into the ground.

Hammer the stake diagonally into the soil behind the tree, just outside the rootball. Nail a special plastic tree tie, which has a collar to prevent it chafing the trunk, to the stake to stop it slipping and buckle it round the tree. Check it now and again to make sure it hasn't become too tight. If you are on a tight budget, you could use a nylon stocking to attach the tree to the stake, but whatever you do don't use wire or nylon twine which will cut into the tree as it grows, and either kill it outright or allow diseases in.

For a larger tree, you can use just two stakes of the same length hammered in vertically either side of the rootball with a cross piece nailed between them. Then nail a tree tie to the cross piece and attach it in the same way.

CARING FOR NEWLY PLANTED TREES

The reason why more than half of all newly planted trees and shrubs die in their first year is no doubt due to lack of water. Young trees are very thirsty and just five minutes with the hose or the odd bucketful of water now and again barely moistens the surface. It takes a long time for soil to be saturated at the lower levels where the roots are, and if you only wet the surface, thirsty roots will come up looking for water there and so be even more susceptible to damage from hot sun or drying winds.

The usual advice – to put the hose (running a bit faster than a trickle but not full-on) on the rootball and leave it for several hours – isn't really applicable any more, given the long, dry summers and hosepipe bans of the last few years. A better solution is to cut a large piece of pipe – flexible or rigid – about 5 cm (2 in) in diameter and as long as the distance between the bottom of the planting hole and the surface of the soil. Bury it next to the rootball when you're planting the tree, leaving the top end of the pipe open on the surface of the soil. Then if we do have another dry summer, one canful of water poured slowly down the pipe will go directly to where it's most needed – around the roots – and will do far more good than three watering cans-full poured on to the soil.

FRAGRANT PLANTS

In a way the front garden is a better place for fragrant plants than the back garden, especially for people who are out at work all day and who at least get the benefit when they go out and come back in. The following plants are all fragrant and suitable for small gardens and, in most cases, for Victorian gardens too.

CLIMBERS

Many scented climbers, like the white *Clematis montana* and the pink flowered 'Elizabeth', are too rampant and too untidy for small front gardens. But the following are suitable, providing you're prepared to hack them back from time to time.

Pink-flowered Jasmine *(Jasminum × stephanense)*

This climber produces pink flowers which are even more sweetly scented than those of the common white jasmine, but it is less vigorous, reaching less than half the height and spread of its relative. It needs sun or part shade and as a twining plant, needs the support of wires or trellis. Or you could grow it through iron railings.
Height and spread: 3 × 3m (10 × 10ft).

Honeysuckle *(Lonicera)*

Among the best varieties are the evergreen *L. japonica* 'Halliana', *L. × americana* with honey-scented flowers, the non-twining, but much less vigorous (only up to 3 m (10 ft) in twenty years) *L. × heckrottii* with a similar scent but with yellow and crimson rather than cream and purple flowers and the early and late Dutch honeysuckles (*L. periclymenum* 'Belgica' and 'Serotina') which between them flower from May to September. Although they are fragrant during the day, the scent is more intense in the evening and at night. Grow them up a tree or on a wall supported by wires or trellis. You can grow *L. × americana* and *L. periclymenum* trained as small standard trees as well.
Average height and spread: 6–7 × 6–7m (20–24 × 20–24ft).

Roses

The ideal climbing rose for a small garden is one that is heavily scented, isn't too vigorous and has a very long flowering period. Among the best are the pink 'Aloha' and the thornless deep cerise 'Zéphirine Drouhin', the yellow 'Maigold' and the apricot-pink 'Compassion'. Up the rose obelisks in one of our Victorian terrace gardens, we grew old favourites like the buff-yellow 'Gloire de Dijon' and the aptly named 'Reine Victoria'. Grow them up the house walls or by the front door and support them with strategically placed lead-headed nails hammered into the wall. If the bricks are very hard, try hammering them into the mortar in between. If that crumbles then replace it and push the lead headed nail into it before it sets, or use one of the plastic self-attaching plant ties.

The tessellated path in our fourth Victorian terrace garden reflects not only
the style of the period, but its owner's love of red and black. The small
rockery and the York stone sunken garden, planted with many different
varieties of ivy, give the garden a Gothic feel.

SHRUBS

Artemisia

These silver leafed foliage plants are excellent for a sunny spot in a well-drained soil. Perhaps the most beautiful is the shrub *A. arborescens* but it's not reliably hardy, so you're better off with one of the tougher perennials like *A. absinthium* 'Lambrook Silver' which has very fine thread-like foliage and grey bobbly flowers, the slightly smaller *A. maritima* 'Powis Castle' which doesn't flower at all or *A. ludoviciana*, which has much more solid, jagged, silver-white leaves. They do retain their leaves through the winter but they look very scruffy by spring, and since the young foliage has the best colour, it's best to cut them back hard each year in early spring. Good for the front of a border is the dwarf *A. schmidtiana* 'Nana' which makes a low hummock of intense silver-grey and which is ideal with red or purple foliage plants.

Average height and spread: 90 × 60 cm (3 × 2 ft). *A. schmidtiana*: 10 × 30 cm (4 × 12 in).

Butterfly bush *(Buddleia davidii, B. fallowiana and B. × 'Loch Inch')*

These are excellent shrubs, if you enjoy seeing butterflies in the garden, since their honey scented flowers act like a magnet for them. Although buddleias respond well to being cut very hard back each year in the spring, even so some of the most widely available varieties are too big for small front gardens. Some of the excellent smaller ones available are *B. fallowiana* 'Alba' with silver foliage and white flowers and *B.* × 'Loch Inch' with silver foliage and soft mauve flowers, neither of which will grow to much more than 1.5 m (5 ft) in a season. Of the new introductions, *B. davidii* 'Nanho Blue', 'Nanho Purple' and 'Nanho White' won't reach much more than 1.2 m (4 ft).

Mexican orange blossom *(Choisya ternata)*

See page 111.

Daphne

A real Victorian favourite, this, and there are several varieties which are suitable for small front gardens, producing between them fragrant flowers from November to August. The best include *D. mezereum* which has very fragrant pale mauve-pink to purple red flowers from January to March, the evergreen *D. odora* with even more fragrant pale pink flowers from February to April (the variegated form *D.o.* 'Aureo-marginata' has the same sweetly scented pink flowers, and because of its variegated foliage is better value in a small garden) and the very small spreading *D. cneorum* which bears fragrant tubular pink flowers in May and June.

Average height and spread: 40 cm–1.8 m × 1 m (15 in–5 ft × 3 ft 3 in).

Lavender (*Lavandula*)

With its narrow silvery foliage and spikes of strongly scented lavender-blue flowers all summer long, this is an ideal shrub to plant by the front door or a path where you are likely to brush against it and release its scent. It can be planted and clipped to make a low informal hedge or edging to a border, or allowed to grow into a rounded bush. Good varieties include the old English lavender (*L. angustifolia*), the dark lavender-blue 'Munstead Dwarf' and the even smaller 'Hidcote' with extremely silvery foliage and intense blue flowers. You can also plant white or pink-flowered lavenders, *L. angustifolia* 'Alba', the dwarf 'Nana Alba' or 'Loddon Pink.' Very fashionable now is French or 'Butterfly' lavender (*L. stoechas* 'Pendunculata') with curious, wispy petals on top of the familiar tight packed flowerheads. There is also a white form *L.s.* 'Alba'.
Height and spread: 30–80 × 30–80 cm (1–2.5 × 1–2.5 ft).

Winter honeysuckle (*Lonicera fragrantissima*)

As its botanical name suggests, this non-climbing shrub has very fragrant small white flowers on almost bare branches (it's semi evergreen) during mild spells from autumn to early spring. In a small garden, maximise its potential by growing through it a small late-flowering clematis like *C. viticella* or *C. texensis* and cut away its spent growth before the honeysuckle comes into flower in late autumn.
Height and spread: 2 × 3 m (6 × 10 ft).

Myrtle (*Myrtus communis*)

In a very warm, sheltered spot this evergreen shrub with strongly scented leaves and small white fluffy flowers born all summer can grow very large, but it is not reliably hardy and can be cut back or even killed by frost. No Victorian bride's bouquet was complete without a sprig of myrtle, which was usually potted up and grown on, so that it could eventually furnish a sprig for the bride's daughter's bouquet.
Height and spread after five years: 2 × 2 m (6 × 6 ft).

Mock orange (*Philadelphus*)
See page 50.

Roses

While there are many excellent scented roses, not many are suitable for a small front garden. None of the new dwarf or patio roses, which would be ideal in size, are noted for their fragrance. Your best bet perhaps is to go for one of the smaller floribundas like the superb blush-white 'Margaret Merril'. Among the smaller-growing English roses, bred by David Austin, 'St Cecilia', 'Kathryn Morley' and 'Pretty Jessica' all have good fragrance.
Average height and spread: 75 × 90 cm (2 ft 6 in × 3 ft).

The formality of the clipped golden privets framing the door contrasts effectively with the informally planted borders.

Rosemary (*Rosmarinus officinalis*)
Another lovely scented plant to grow in a sunny spot by the front door. Choose one of the smaller varieties like *R.o.* 'Benenden Blue' or the even smaller 'Severn Sea'.
Average height and spread: 40–80 cm × 50 cm – 1 m (16–32 in × 20 in–3 ft).

Cotton lavender (*Santolina chamaecyparissus*)
This plant with pretty aromatic silver foliage thrives in a hot dry spot and, with a little judicious clipping, forms an attractive round shape. You will lose the flowers that way but since they are a brassy yellow that is no great loss. The less common *S. neapolitana* has equally attractive silvery foliage and much more attractive pale yellow flowers. There is also a good green santolina, *S. virens* or *viridis*, with bright green foliage and lemon yellow flowers.
Average height and spread: 50 cm × 1 m (18 in × 1 ft).

Lilac (*Syringa*)
Another Victorian favourite but the only forms really suitable for a small front garden are the very small slow growing Korean lilac (*S. meyeri* 'Palibin' or 'Velutina') with masses of sweetly scented pink-lilac flowers in May or June and the slightly larger Littleleaf lilac (*S. microphylla*) which flowers in early summer and then sometimes again in autumn.
Average height and spread: 1.2–1.5 m × 80–90 cm (4–5 ft × 2 ft 6 in–3 ft).

Viburnum

This family includes in its large and varied ranks many of the most sweetly scented shrubs of all, but most of them are really too big for the very small front garden. If you have got space, though, winter scented *V.* × *bodnantense* 'Dawn' is superb, as is the evergreen *V. tinus* 'Eve Price'. For spring fragrance look for the evergreen (or semi-evergreen in some areas) *V.* × *burkwoodii* 'Park Farm Hybrid' which is good trained against a sheltered wall, the smaller deciduous *V. carlesii* with pink-budded white flowers smelling like pinks and *V.* × *juddii* with exquisitely scented pale pink flowers in late spring.
Average height and spread: 1.5–2 × 1.2–1.5 m (5–6 × 4–5 ft).

HERBACEOUS PLANTS

Lily-of-the-valley (*Convallaria majalis*)
No self-respecting Victorian front garden would have been without its lily-of-the-valley. This good ground-covering plant does best in part shade. You often see it today, growing in those narrow beds between the front path and the party wall.
Height and spread: 20 × 50 + cm (8 × 20 + in).

Pinks (*Dianthus*)
This large family, in its many forms – Chinese pinks, Cheddar pinks, Maiden pinks, Border pinks – was a great Victorian favourite. They all love hot dry alkaline soils. Of the lower-growing varieties look for hybrids like 'Little Jock', 'Nyewoods Cream' and 'Pikes Pink'. For the taller varieties see page 53. The mat-forming types like *D. deltoides* 'Flashing Light' (salmon-red flowers), 'Samos' (carmine) and 'Brighteyes' (white with a red eye) look good growing over a low wall.
Height and spread: 10–30 × 25–75 cm (4 in–1 ft × 9 in–2.5 ft).

Lemon balm (*Melissa officinalis*)
See page 64.

Evening Primrose (*Oenothera*)
The best form for scent is *O. biennis* whose deep yellow flowers open at dusk, as do those of the perennial *O. odorata* (or *O. stricta*) although this is much harder to find. These are both tall-growing – to about 3 ft (90 cm) – so for the front of a border look for *O. missouriensis* which is much lower-growing but sadly doesn't have the same fragrance as its relatives.
Height and spread: 25–90 × 60 cm (10 in–3 ft × 2 ft).

Thyme (*Thymus*)
Another herb which is a good all-round garden plant for a well-drained soil and a sunny spot, it boasts attractive foliage and pretty minute flowers all summer long as well as having a wonderful smell. Plant it by the path, where it's likely to get brushed against, if not trodden on, and release its scent. Good mat-forming varieties include the dark green and gold variegated *T.*'Doone Valley', the bright gold 'Golden Carpet' and the silver-leafed *T. praecox arcticus* 'Pink Chintz'. They are all widely available.
Height and spread: 5 × 30 cm (2 in × 1 ft).

ANNUALS

Some of the most popular annuals with Victorian gardeners were very strongly scented. They all flower from June to September or, in some cases, until the first frosts. The half-hardy annuals, which need to be sown under glass or bought as plants from the garden centre, are marked HH.

Alyssum (*A. maritimum* now known as *Lobularia maritima*)
This very easily grown annual has a scent some people describe as like new-mown hay.
Height and spread: 10 × 30 cm (4 × 12 in).

Sweet William (*Dianthus barbatus*)
This has several biennial and annual forms which have a fragrance slightly reminiscent of cloves. Look for the biennial 'Auricula-eyed' form, with bi-coloured red or pink and white flowers or one of the annual dwarf mixtures like 'Roundabout' or 'Wee Willie'.
Height and spread: 15–45 × 15–30 cm (6–18 in × 6 in–1 ft).

Cherry Pie (*Heliotropium*)
This classic Victorian half-hardy annual has large clusters of deep violet-blue flowers with a heady rather fruity scent, hence its common name. 'Marine' and 'Mini Marine' are good varieties, the latter a few inches shorter than the former. Grow it in hanging baskets as well as in borders and raise the fragrance to nose level!
Height and spread: 45–50 × 30 cm (16–18 × 12 in) HH.

Sweet peas (*Lathyrus*)
You can grow sow the seed directly into the soil where they are to flower, but you almost always get better results from seed sown under glass the previous autumn or early spring. If you have no greenhouse, then it's probably better to buy young plants from the garden centre. There are hundreds of different sweet peas to choose from, in many different

shades, so it's worth buying a strongly scented variety. Grow them on trellis, or woven through railings as an informal annual hedge.

Height and spread: up to 3 × 2 m (10 × 6 ft).

Stocks (Matthiola)

This is a superbly scented family of showy spring and summer flowering cottage garden annuals and biennials in shades of white, yellow, pink, mauve, lavender and red. Ten week stock (*Matthiola*) is a half-hardy annual, while Brompton stock (*Matthiola incana*) is a biennial. Virginian stocks (*Malcolmia maritima*) are easily grown hardy annuals with small flowers in white pink or mauve, while night scented stock (*Matthiola bicornis*) is a hardy annual whose small flowers are insignificant but whose fragrance at night should guarantee it a place among the more attractive-looking stocks.

Height and spread: 30–50 cm (1–1.5 ft).

Tobacco plants (Nicotiana)

These are all scented though, with the exception of a mixture called 'Evening Fragrance', the many coloured modern hybrids are not as sweetly scented, particularly in the evenings, as the taller white *N. affinis*. If you can find it, the short-lived perennial *N. sylvestris*, which can reach almost 2 m (6 ft) in height, also has superb fragrance in the evening.

Height: 30–75 cm (1 ft–2 ft 6 in).

BULBS

Lilies (Lilium)

The white *L. regale* has a stunning fragrance on warm days that seems to intensify in the evening, so even though it is probably too large for a very small front garden it is well worth trying to fit it in. You could try it at the back of a sunny border where the plants in front can shade its roots, or you could grow a few in a tub and move them to the back garden once they've finished flowering.

Height: 1 m (3 ft).

Narcissi

One of the most sweetly scented is the white narcissus 'Cheerfulness' while other good varieties for fragrance include the jonquil narcissi like 'Trevithian', 'Lintie', 'Suzy' and *Narcissus × odorus* 'Rugulosus Plenus' (much more attractive than its name!) and the old 'Pheasant's Eye' (*N. poeticus recurvus*) with its white petals and distinctive red and gold 'eye'.

Height: 15–30 cm (6–12 in).

THE COTTAGE GARDEN

*W*hen you mention an English front garden, the image that's most likely to spring to mind is of a traditional country cottage garden that's both decorative and productive where herbs and flowers – lavender, foxgloves, sweet pea and stock – jostle for space among the fruit and vegetables. To add to this rural and romantic picture, roses and honeysuckle climb the thatch.

The cottage garden is so much a part of our vision of Olde England that we assume it has been around for hundreds of years. But in fact, as explained by Anne Scott James in her book *The Cottage Garden* (Penguin 1982), what we understand by this plot of ground around a labourer's cottage which not only grew flowers but had to produce enough vegetables and meat, almost always in the form of a pig, to feed a family, really only came into being during the Regency period and the earlier part of Queen Victoria's reign.

At least, that would appear to be the case, because there is no evidence that the cottage garden existed earlier than the mid-eighteenth century. In fact, you would have to dig deep to find a clear description of any ordinary garden before that time. Although writers and artists of the time left us such vivid accounts of the grand houses with their acres of magnificent gardens, they neglected to record the homes and gardens of ordinary people, which were obviously considered to be of no interest whatsoever!

Our knowledge is further hampered by the fact that the meaning of the word 'cottage' has changed in the last two hundred years. Before the mid-eighteenth century, a 'cottager' wasn't a labourer but a small farmer or a craftsman, like a blacksmith, and a cottage was a substantial house.

A good place to look for clues about original cottage gardens is the Weald and Downland Open Air Museum at Singleton in West Sussex where they have rebuilt a fifteenth-century farmhouse, complete with mediaeval 'cottage' garden. The Bayleaf Farmhouse garden is laid out on a grid system with small, rectangular beds edged with grass paths and filled with vegetables like peas, leeks, onions and 'worts' (the brassicas which made up the 'pottage' or vegetable stew that was the staple diet in mediaeval England), and features lots of herbs, both culinary and medicinal. But although it is primarily a productive garden, it isn't purely utilitarian: in mid-summer, when many of the herbs are in flower, it's also a riot of colour.

In Elizabethan times, as prosperity increased, many of these 'cottage' gardens grew purely ornamental flowers as well as herbs and vegetables, and the ornamental content increased with the introduction of 'florists' flowers' like auriculas, pinks, ranunculus and tulips which were grown by amateur enthusiasts known as 'florists'.

In the eighteenth century, many rich landowners enclosed their land to create newly fashionable landscaped parks. If a village or hamlet spoilt the view, then the houses were sometimes pulled down and the luckier tenants rehoused in model villages of small cottages with gardens. Since wages were so low these small plots had to be used to feed the family, growing mainly vegetables, herbs, and only if space permitted, a few flowers, either taken from the wild or grown from seed given by the gardener at the big house.

During the second half of the eighteenth century another new type of 'cottager' appeared – impoverished members of the gentry going down in the world, who either improved existing cottages or built new ones and became enthusiastic gardeners. By about 1825, the two streams of cottage gardening, the subsistence and the romantic, met and in the process created the lovely and productive cottage garden we know today.

There were two main styles of cottage garden. In the first, the house was close to the road and the small front garden, called the 'forecourt', was given over to flowers while the much larger area at the back grew produce. In the other, the one we think of as a typical cottage garden, most of the land was at the front of the house with a long narrow path between front gate and front door. Here flowers would be grown under the windows and close to the path on either side with the fruit and vegetables behind. The chickens, the pig and the privy were confined to the smaller area out at the back!

The basic principle of growing many different types of plants in a colourful but ordered jumble adapts well to many front gardens today. The cottage garden has the added advantage, once the plants are established, of needing relatively little maintenance and, provided you cheat a little by including a few more evergreens than you might otherwise do, it can be colourful all year round.

Our cottage garden

The cottage was over three hundred years old, a long, low building painted white with exposed beams stained black. Its owners, Karen and Andy O'Neill, who have two young daughters, had bought it eighteen months earlier and had spent most of that time working on the house itself. Now that the house was more or less in order, they were ready to start on the garden.

It was a decent-sized garden, 70ft wide × 20ft deep facing south-west and running mainly along the front of the cottage with a strip up the side. The path of concrete slabs ran from the wrought iron front gate to the front door, set back into a deep porch.

Like the house, the garden had been rather neglected over the years, although there were some positive features, such as a good stretch of wall and a holly hedge. A small magnolia, a couple of fruit trees and a few clumps of primulas were also worth saving.

On the downside, there were a few old shrub and hybrid tea roses which were either too spindly to keep or not appropriate for a cottage garden, a couple of old woody hydrangeas that were past their best and, in the south-west corner, a young weeping willow, about 15 ft high and about the same distance from the house. The rest was rough, tussocky grass. In another corner stood a common feature of the modern cottage garden – a large green oil storage tank on metal legs!

The O'Neills felt so daunted by the task that they hadn't got much further than a few vague thoughts. They knew they would like a cottage garden in keeping with the style of the house, an area for the children, somewhere to put the whirly washing line and some space for entertaining.

Designer Ryl Nowell, who has won gold medals for her cottage gardens at the Chelsea Flower Show, was excited by the challenge of the O'Neills' garden. Immediately she felt that the cottage and garden didn't relate to each other: the newly painted building seemed a bit clinical and urban and isolated from the garden which was very rural in feel. Her overall aim was to marry the two.

The first thing Ryl wanted to do was make more of the entrance, to take away the small wrought iron gate, more suitable for a suburban semi than a country cottage, and replace it with a white picket gate, and a white wooden arch to support climbing roses. This would also create more privacy, by screening the garden off from the adjacent lane.

The front door was a problem. It was in the newer, less attractive extension, and well-hidden at the back of the porch. Since the oldest part of the cottage, to the left of the front door, was also the prettiest, with bow windows and a glazed door, Ryl decided to focus on that. She created a path through what will be tall, dense planting on either side

Left: The new white gate and arch in our cottage garden frames the entrance perfectly. *Below:* The view from the front door back up the garden to the gate.

drawing your eye, and your steps, towards the most attractive part of the cottage, and then diverting you back towards the front door.

The planting, truly 'cottagey' in feel, included a mixture of shrubs like buddleia, holly, hydrangea, lavatera, hibiscus, lavender, and, of course, roses. There were herbaceous perennials such as alchemilla, campanula, foxgloves, hollyhocks, honesty and lupins and annuals like sweet peas and sunflowers. Herbs included rosemary, thyme, sage, fennel and golden oreganum while vegetables like courgettes and the lovely old red-and-white-flowered runner bean 'Painted Lady' added to the cottage garden feel, and were invaluable as space fillers in the newly planted borders.

The area to the left of the path – a large patch of rough grass – seemed ideal for the children's play area since it was right outside the kitchen window. Ryl incorporated a sandpit which would become a formal pool when the children were older. She positioned the whirly washing line there too, devising a tent which simply slipped over the framework when there was no washing on it to create a playhouse for the children.

Ryl solved the problem of the oil storage tank by screening off that small corner of the garden with a simple picket fence curving upwards in the centre to disguise the highest part of the tank, and put in a gate for access. We stained the woodwork a lovely Iris blue, the perfect foil for the plants – runner beans this year, probably a golden hop the year after – and used some of the now dead space behind the fence for the compost heap.

The area behind the large cottage garden border seemed the perfect place for entertaining, since it was the south-west-facing corner of the garden and got the best of the evening sun. So we decided to put a patio and a lawn there. The area to the side of the house, which, on the plan, had steps and a pergola, Andy and Karen decided to make 'Phase Two', to be done next year, when time and money allowed. On the paving by the front door, we put a few terracotta pots, containing petunias and lobelia in the same pinky-mauve shades, along with one Ali Baba pot whose shape was so strong that it looked great unplanted. Andy and Karen were utterly delighted with the garden, and Andy had so enjoyed working on it that he felt gardening would now be a major interest – as long as it didn't conflict too much with the football season!

Cottage garden plants

To create an authentic look, it's best to use old-fashioned cottage garden plants, though there is no reason not to use modern hybrids, with all their advantages of more vigorous growth, longer flowering season and disease resistance, provided the essential character of the plants is the same. The modern hybrid delphiniums, for instance either the Belladonna, Pacific or New Century strains, come in the traditional range of blues (avoid the white, pink, or heaven forbid, red delphiniums!). Old roses, another cottage garden staple, are superb for scent, flower colour and form, but many only flower for a short time and are often too large, lax and rambling for today's smaller gardens. A better bet would be the new English roses, bred by David Austin, which have the subtle colours, intricate petal patterns and perfume of the old roses, but flower all through the summer, are smaller, neater plants and have better disease-resistance too. Hybrid teas, on the other hand, with their rather unattractive stiff habit and sometimes garish modern flower colours, would not do.

TREES

Apple trees
If you don't inherit any old gnarled ones, choose those on dwarfing rootstocks; M 26 or M 106 are probably the most suitable for small gardens, though be prepared to stake them, and to feed and water them well unless you have very fertile soil. Grow as bushes or dwarf pyramids.

Holly
The birds often brought holly seed into a cottage garden, where it may well have been clipped into some sort of geometric shape. For small gardens choose *Ilex aquifolium* 'Pyramidalis', which has attractive glossy green leaves and an interesting shape. It is also self-fertile.

Yew
Although yew is associated much more with grand houses and vast expanses of hedge, it was a popular cottage garden specimen plant, often clipped into a topiary shape.

HEDGES

A few cottage gardens had yew hedges, but quickthorn or hawthorn was more common. Once 'laid' (and there are still skilled countrymen around who can 'lay' a hedge) it provided an animal-proof barrier – vital since your family's survival could be threatened if the crops in your garden were trampled or eaten. Other hedges, planted by nature, were trees and shrubs like hawthorn, blackthorn, elder and wild rose.

Hawthorn (*Crataegus monogyna*)
Probably still the best for a real country cottage garden.

Mixed hedge
Imitate nature <u>and</u> provide a wildlife habitat by planting several native species like Elder (*Sambucus nigra*), Rugosa roses, Hazel (*Corylus*) and Guelder Rose (*Viburnum opulus*) together.

In a small cottage garden, box might be a good choice, though make sure it's *Buxus sempervirens* and not *Buxus sempervirens* 'Suffruticosa', the dwarf box.

The shrubby honeysuckle (*Lonicera nitida* or the golden leafed variety *L. nitida* 'Baggesen's Gold') is a good choice, although it's faster growing than box and so needs clipping more regularly.

Privet was sometimes used in cottage gardens, but is best avoided in any small garden because it is such a greedy feeder, sucking all the moisture and nutrients out of the soil around it and making it very hard to grow anything else close by.

CLIMBERS AND WALL SHRUBS

No self-respecting cottage would deem itself worthy of the name unless it had roses (or at the very least honeysuckle) around the door! And because every inch of space was precious, cottagers often grew shrubs against the cottage walls too.

Japonica (*Chaenomeles japonica*)
The bright red flowers provide a splash of welcome colour during late winter/early spring and of course the quinces produced in the autumn made good jelly. The *C. speciosa* hybrids like 'Moerloosii' and 'Nivalis' can be trained on walls, while the *C.* × *superba* hybrids like 'Knap Hill Scarlet' with large translucent red flowers and 'Fire Dance' with bright scarlet blooms, make excellent free standing shrubs.

Clematis
Many of the more modern hybrids would look out of place in a cottage garden, but some of the earliest ones like the rich, purple flowered 'Jackmanii', which was raised and first

Left: The simple white picket fence is the perfect foil for the bright red and gold poppies. *Below:* In this cottage garden the white roses and marguerites give a cool sophisticated look. *Right:* Even in the smallest space, old-fashioned favourites like marguerites and hollyhocks can create a cottage garden effect.

offered for sale in 1862 by the famous Jackman nurseries in Surrey, or the white flowered 'Henryi' and 'Miss Bateman', introduced soon after, would be ideal. Even more traditional, the native Virgin's Bower (*C. flammula*) has thousands of small, sweetly scented white flowers in late summer/early autumn, and will scramble happily through a tree or hedge.

Clematis montana is probably too vigorous, although I have seen it grown to perfection in one cottage garden, almost as a hedge, twining through hooped iron railings dividing the garden from the road.

Ivy (*Hedera*)

A plant that found its way into many cottage gardens from the woodland around but one that shouldn't be despised on that account. Indeed, for a very shady spot such as a north-facing wall or one in the lee of another building which gets no sun at all there really is nothing better. It's also attractive grown up a tree, or as ground cover in difficult places like the poor, dry soil under large trees. There are so many to choose from but it's safer to stick with the native *Hedera helix* varieties or the Irish Ivy *H. hibernica* rather than go for one of the Persian ivies *H. colchica* whose very large leaves might look out of scale on the walls of a small cottage.

Jasmine (*Jasminum officinale*)

This very untidy climber with its wonderfully sweet-scented white flowers is another traditional cottage garden plant that will twine round the door or even up into an old tree.

Everlasting pea (*Lathyrus latifolius*)

This perennial relative of the much more showy sweet pea is easy to grow, and was often found near the front door. It looks like a pea in its growth, will reach 2m (6ft 6in) or more and has masses of pinkish-purple pea flowers. There is also a very desirable white-flowered form, if you can find it. Both are relatively easy to grow from seed.

Honeysuckle (*Lonicera periclymenum*)

Even if you have no other climbers in your cottage garden you must have honeysuckle, either growing round the door, on a fence or up an old tree. The best for this purpose are undoubtedly varieties bred from the native woodbine, such as *L.p.* 'Belgica' (or early Dutch honeysuckle) which has strongly scented pale rose-purple and yellow flowers from May to June and 'Serotina' (or late Dutch honeysuckle) which has equally deliciously scented but darker-coloured flowers from July to October.

Passionflower (*Passiflora caerulea*)

Grown against a warm sheltered wall, in a warmer part of the country, this exotic-looking climber is almost evergreen and even if the top growth is cut back by a hard frost chances are that, if the base has been protected with straw, it will shoot again in spring.

Roses

Roses round the door, or at the very least growing over an archway above the gate, are an almost essential ingredient of cottage gardens. One of the most popular ramblers was 'Gloire de Dijon', generally known as 'Old Glory', 'Yellow Glory' or just plain 'Glory'. Its richly scented flowers are a subtle biscuity-apricot colour, which explains its popularity with smart gardeners today. At its best in June, although it does flower intermittently throughout the summer.

The thornless, repeat-flowering cerise-pink 'Zéphirine Drouhin' is another good choice, as is its beautiful pale pink sport 'Kathleen Harrop'. 'Mme Alfred Carrière' is another traditional favourite with its clusters of white flowers which appear in June and then intermittently throughout the summer.

Vines (*Vitis*)

During the golden age of the cottage garden, many cottages in the south of England were covered with productive vines. These provided not only attractive foliage throughout the summer and autumn, but also grapes for the table and for wine-making. In mild areas, and if you have a south-facing house wall, it's still possible to do the same with a hardy variety like 'Müller-Thurgau' or 'Brandt'. If you don't live in a mild area or can't be bothered with training a grape vine you can achieve a similar effect with an ornamental vine like the large-leafed *V. coignetiae* (the Japanese crimson glory vine), which has spectacular autumn colour, or even with Virginia creeper. The best variety is *Parthenocissus henryana* which has deep velvety green leaves veined with silver in summer as well as the usual autumn firework display of reds, oranges and golds.

SHRUBS

Broom (*Cytisus*)

Very popular low-growing shrubs flowering in late spring/early summer. Old hybrids like *C.* × *praecox*, with its masses of pale yellow pea flowers, *C.* × *praecox* 'Allgold', with much deeper golden yellow flowers and *C.* × *kewensis* with creamy white flowers are still among the best available.

Deutzia

These very free-flowering shrubs come in a range of sizes from the tall *D. scabra* 'Pride of Rochester' with blush white double flowers which reaches 2m (6ft 6in) or more to *D.* × *rosea* with clear pink flowers, which won't reach more than 80cm (2ft 8in).

Fuchsia

The hardy members of the family like 'Mrs Popple', 'Riccartonii' and 'Tom Thumb', with small bright red, or red and purple flowers, are very useful small late-summer-flowering shrubs.

St John's Wort (*Hypericum calycinum*)

This was traditionally grown in cottage gardens for its medicinal properties but while its large buttercup-like golden flowers are very attractive it is so invasive that it's best avoided in a small garden. A better bet, though less authentic, is *H. patulum* 'Hidcote', a taller shrub with similar golden flowers, but without its relative's bad habits!

Lavender

Another 'must' for any cottage garden, not only for its old-fashioned associations, but for the wonderful hazy blue of its flowers, its evergreen grey foliage and its abilities to attract bees and butterflies. The 'Old English' lavender *Lavandula angustifolia* grows to 80 × 80cm (2ft 6in × 2ft 6in) while 'Twickel Purple', which is just a bit smaller, forms an attractive rounded bush and holds the flowers well clear of the foliage. But for a small space 'Hidcote', with the deepest blue flowers of all and a full height of 30cm (1ft), is probably your best bet.

The front gardens above are minute, but filled with colourful roses they brighten up what would otherwise be rather bleak stone cottages.

The planting on either side of the path (*right*) demonstrates how effective keeping to just three colours – in this case blue-mauve, gold and white – can be, and the white walls set them off to perfection.

Mock orange blossom (*Philadelphus*)

As its common name suggests, this shrub became a favourite because of its white flowers with their rich heady fragrance in early summer. It can grow into an extremely large shrub so look out for one of the smaller growing varieties like 'Belle Etoile', 'Innocence' or, smallest of all, 'Manteau d'Hermine'.

Roses

No cottage garden would be complete without old-fashioned roses with evocative names like 'Blush Damask', 'Maiden's Blush' and 'Roseraie de l'Hay'. Unfortunately, most only flower for a few weeks or grow too large for most small gardens. A good compromise would be the new 'English' roses which combine the compact habit, repeat flowering, vigour and disease resistance of modern roses with the lovely soft colours and scent of the old varieties. Perhaps the best yellow is still 'Graham Thomas', while there are any number of wonderful soft pinks, like 'Claire Rose' or, for a hint of apricot, 'Heritage'.

Lilac (*Syringa vulgaris*)

One of the most popular cottage garden shrubs with its fresh green leaves and clusters of sweet scented flowers in early summer. Although there are lots of modern hybrids with flowers in a wide range of colours from pale pink to wine red the traditional colour is, well, lilac – and possibly white. The problem with the common lilac is that it grows very large – over 6 × 6 m (20 × 20 ft) and although you can cut it back, it could take two or three years to flower again. Your best bet might be to go for a smaller-growing hybrid, either the lilac-flowered *S.v.* 'Michel Buchner' or the white-flowering *S.v.* 'Vestale'.

HERBACEOUS PLANTS

Lady's mantle (*Alchemilla mollis*)

Although this plant has sprays of sulphur yellow flowers all summer long, it is worth growing for its beautiful fan-like, pale green leaves. It seeds itself with reckless abandon so just pull it up where you don't want it.

Pearl everlasting (*Anaphalis triplinervis* 'Summer Snow')

This carries clusters of pearly-white everlasting daisies above spreading clumps of grey foliage between July and September.

Columbine or Granny's bonnets (*Aquilegia vulgaris*)

These beautiful, nodding, early summer flowers come in a range of bright colours including cream, red and yellow and are sometimes bi-coloured. They self-seed freely and also self-hybridise so if you have one you are particularly fond of, propagate it by division in the autumn rather than rely on seedlings.

Michaelmas daisies (*Aster amellus*)

These are a must for autumn colour in any cottage garden. Although the tall ones now come in other colours including white and pink, purists plump for the traditional blue-mauve. The old variety 'King George' is still one of the best. Dwarf Michaelmas daisies (*A. novi-belgii*) are also cloaked in many colours but again the mauve-blue 'Audrey' and soft lavender-mauve 'Lady in Blue' are traditional.

Double daisy (*Bellis perennis*)

This plant with lots of pretty double flowers in early summer is an old favourite dating back to the sixteenth century. Good varieties include 'Dresden China' with shell pink flowers, 'Alice' with peachy-pink flowers and the intriguing 'Hen and Chicken', *B.p.* 'Prolifera', where a ring of miniature daisies hang from the central one.

Campanula

Along with delphiniums, hollyhocks and foxgloves, the very tall campanulas like *C. lactiflora* which can reach 1.5m (5ft) or more provide the strong vertical lines which are such a feature of cottage garden planting. This particular variety has such large heads of powder blue flowers that it really needs staking if it isn't going to flop, so smaller varieties like the blue or white *C. latifolia*, or *C. persicifolia* which produce stiff stems from neat rosettes of narrow evergreen leaves, are a better bet.

The dwarf campanulas are excellent for the front of a border, because they flower for months, spilling over on to the path. Some of the excellent modern hybrids including the blue *C. carpatica* 'Chewton Joy', 'Isobel', 'Blue Moonlight' and 'Bressingham White' are a bit too modern for a traditional cottage garden, while the Wall Harebell (*C. portenschlagiana*, syn. *C. muralis*) is more in keeping though rampant. However, you can control it easily enough by ripping it out when it's gone far enough!

Chrysanthemum (*Argyranthemum, Dendranthemum* or *Leucanthemum*)

Chrysanthemums (as they used to be called before the botanists divided them up and changed their names) found their way into the cottage garden as 'florist's flowers'. They provide invaluable white 'daisies' for the cottage garden, flowering from mid summer to autumn. Good varieties include the tall *L. × superbum* 'Wirral Supreme' and 'Snowcap' which is little more than half its size. For a splash of colour in late summer try the rich mahogany red *D.* 'Duchess of Edinburgh' and the pale apricot-yellow, *D.* 'Mary Stoker'.

Delphinium

Probably the most spectacular blue-flowered cottage garden plants of all, and now that there are dwarf varieties available they are suitable for the smallest garden. Look for Belladonna hybrids like 'Lamartine', 'Peace', 'Blue Bees' and the Pacific hybrids or New Century hybrids, plus the even smaller dwarf hybrids like 'Blue Fountains' and 'Blue Heaven'. Stick to blue and don't be seduced by the pinks or whites!

The main problems in growing delphiniums are that they'll rot if the soil is too wet and heavy and that slugs love the young leaves. If you don't want to use slug pellets, then 10cm (4in) rings cut from plastic soft drinks bottles and pushed well into the soil around each young plant are a very effective deterrent.

Pinks (*Dianthus*)

These were grown in mediaeval monastery gardens and used in Elizabethan recipes for their clove scent. The cottage pinks were 'florists' flowers' and many excellent heavily scented hybrids were bred in the eighteenth and nineteenth centuries, including 'Charles Musgrave', 'Bridal Veil', 'Inchmery', 'Mrs Sinkins' and 'Sam Barlow'. Unfortunately, they have a relatively short flowering period but the more modern hybrids like the Allwoodii pinks or the new 'Devon' range flower for much longer.

Foxglove (*Digitalis purpurea*)
Another 'must' for a cottage garden, this very obliging plant will grow in deep shade and, although strictly speaking a biennial, it will seed itself so freely that, once you've got it, you'll never be without it! Purists grow the native purple-flowered species, but would probably allow the lovely white form *D.p.* 'Alba'.

Crane's-bill (*Geranium*)
Not to be confused with the bedding and pot varieties (*Pelargonium*) – although no cottage garden would be complete without a pot or two of those, either – crane's-bills come in all shapes and sizes with flowers ranging from white through the blues and pinks to fluorescent magenta and a purple so deep it's almost black. See page 153 for details.

Avens (*Geum*)
An easy-to-grow plant, forming slowly-spreading clumps of rich green rounded leaves, although the soft coppery pink flowers of *G. rivale* or the coppery-orange of *G. × borisii* might be more suitable here than hybrids like the bright yellow 'Lady Stratheden' and the brick-red 'Mrs Bradshaw'.

Baby's breath (*Gypsophila*)
This plant produces sprays of tiny white flowers all through the summer months. Its botanical name means 'chalk lover' because it thrives on chalky soil and hates acid soil. The best white form is 'Bristol White' and there's a very pretty pink one called 'Rosy Veil'.

Christmas rose (*Helleborus niger*)
It rarely blooms at Christmas but is a welcome winter-flowering plant in any cottage garden with its leathery evergreen leaves and simple pure white flowers.

Day lilies (*Hemerocallis*)
The flowers only last for a day but they are produced in such profusion over many weeks that it doesn't matter. They also produce weed-smothering clumps of bright green strap-like leaves. There are many different hybrids (there is even a Hemerocallis Society) but go for good traditional ones like *H. fulva* with sweetly scented yellow flowers or the equally fragrant pale primrose 'Whichford' and the warm peachy-pink 'Pink Damask'.

Sweet rocket (*Hesperis matronalis*)
This old favourite has large clusters of mauve or white flowers which have the most delicious fragrance in the evening.

Left: You can achieve a profuse cottage-garden look very effectively on a hard surface by using containers, and of course it gives you the opportunity to change the display with the seasons.

Iris

Again, no self-respecting cottage garden could be without irises – another of the original 'florists' flowers'. Choose either flag irises (*I. germanica*), bearded irises which need a very sunny spot, or the more delicate *I. sibirica* which will thrive in a sunny spot, provided the soil is moist. Look for *I.s.* 'Alba' and 'Flight of Butterflies' with rich blue flowers distinctively veined in white, or 'Papillon' with flowers of the softest blue. For winter flowering, there's *I. stylosa* with lavender-blue flowers.

Red hot pokers (*Kniphofia*)

As their name suggests, their flowers glow orange or red, but new strains come with ivory flowers, green in bud ('Little Maid') and cream flowers, red in bud ('Strawberries and Cream'). If you plant them in autumn protect them from frost in their first winter with a heap of bracken or straw.

Peonies (*Paeonia*)

Another cottage garden classic, particularly the old deep red *P. officinalis*, which everyone's granny had in her garden. There are many other good peony varieties available like *P. lactiflora* 'Baroness Schroeder' (white), *P. l.* 'Albert Crousse' (pink) and 'Felix Crousse' (red). Sadly, they take up a lot of space, only flower for a short time and their foliage is nothing to write home about, so they need to be surrounded with plants that will make up for their deficiencies the rest of the summer.

Oriental poppies (*Papaver orientale*)

Nothing quite matches these big blowsy flowers in their traditional brilliant orange-scarlet colour but they now come in many other colours including pink, mauve and even black and white! Poppies are inclined to flop, but the joy of cottage garden planting is that everything grows so closely together that, in the words of Christopher Lloyd, the plants can all support each other like drunks after a party! The foliage may start to die off in mid-summer so be sure to plant them next to or behind something that flowers later. Alternatively, cut the foliage back, and fill the temporary gaps with plants in pots.

Phlox (*P. paniculata*)

A must for any self-respecting cottage garden with its bright long-lasting flowers in many hues. Good, widely available varieties include 'Balmoral', 'Border Gem', 'Prince of Orange' and 'White Admiral'. Phlox is not the ideal plant for weekend cottage gardeners because it suffers badly in very dry weather.

Jacob's ladder (*Polemonium*)

The common name comes from its ladder-like bright green foliage. It has clusters of mid-blue flowers throughout the summer and once established, will seed itself freely, but you can easily hoe it out if it becomes a nuisance.

Primula

A whole range of primulas had their place in the traditional cottage garden, from the showy auriculas, a popular 'florists' flower', along with polyanthus, cowslips and the lovely soft yellow native primrose, which was originally dug up from the wild and transplanted in the garden. Good, low-growing plants for moist partly-shaded places.

London pride (*Saxifraga umbrosa*)

Its rosettes of leathery evergreen leaves, together with its early summer sprays of pale pink flowers on long stems, make it a good plant for edging a sunny path, although it likes a little protection from the midday sun.

Mullein (*Verbascum*)

Perhaps the most spectacular member of the family is *V. olympicum*, with huge silver felt-like leaves and spikes of small yellow flowers almost 2 m (6 ft) tall. Possibly more manageable is the smaller hybrid 'Gainsborough' which has greener foliage and bigger softer yellow flowers. They all need very free-draining soil or they will rot.

Sweet violet (*Viola odorata*)

In late winter/early spring, these are smothered in very sweetly-scented flowers of violet or white. They form very low-growing clumps and so are ideal for edging a path or border. Look for *V.o.* 'Alba', 'The Czar', 'Princess of Wales', or one of the Parma violets like 'Duchesse de Parme'.

Pansies (*Viola tricolor*)

Another species where the plant breeders have produced a vast number of new varieties in different colours. Good, more traditional varieties still around include 'Ardross Gem', deep blue with gold centres, 'Irish Molly', a curious mixture of chestnut, khaki, olive green and gold, and 'Maggie Mott' with large lilac and pale blue petals.

BIENNIALS

These are plants that grow from seed one year and go on to flower the next.

Hollyhocks (*Althaea rosea*)

Any cottage garden depicted on a biscuit tin or a tray cloth will be bound to have some stately hollyhocks beside the cottage door! Varieties like 'Chater's Double Mixed' can reach 2–2.6 m (6–8 ft) in height and flower between June and September. The problem is that they are very susceptible to rust which disfigures the foliage. The only answer is to keep your fingers crossed – or grow a variety like 'Summer Carnival' which will flower in its first year.

Wallflowers (*Cheiranthus cheiri*)

Although it's possible to buy seeds of mixed colours, it's much better to buy single colours like 'Blood Red', 'Cloth of Gold' or 'Fire King Improved' and decide on the grouping of colours yourself.

Sweet William (*Dianthus barbatus*)

Part of its charm is the mixture of colours, reds, pinks and those with a contrasting white eye or ring. Good varieties include 'Indian Carpet' and 'Auricula-Eyed Mixed'.

Honesty (*Lunaria*)

It's really the flat, round, papery white seed heads – ideal for indoor winter arrangements – rather than the mauve flowers that make honesty worth growing. The new white-flowered variety is even more attractive.

Forget-me-not (*Myosotis*)

Although now available in pink and white, it's the true forget-me-not blue that you're after, like 'Ultramarine'. It also seeds itself all over the place, so it's yours for life. Just pull up any seedlings that are surplus to requirements.

Evening primrose (*Oenothera biennis*)

The biennial form of the tall, yellow-flowered evening primrose has the best perfume of the whole family, especially at night. It's not that easy to find but is worth tracking down, as seed or a young plant. Another plant that self-sows with abandon.

ANNUALS

Alyssum

A good cottage garden plant because it seeds itself so freely that you only ever have to buy one packet of seeds! 'Carpet of Snow' and 'Snow Crystals', with the largest flowers yet, are both good choices.

Snapdragon (*Antirrhinum*)

The traditional kind grow to 90cm–1.2m (3–4ft) and although the breeders have come up with some excellent dwarf varieties like 'Magic Carpet' it's hard to get them in single colours. A good compromise might be the intermediate varieties like

Right: Although topiary is usually associated with grand, rather formal
gardens, it was a common feature of the traditional cottage garden
too, often a self-seeded yew or a holly would be clipped into a geometric shape.

the 'Monarch' range which reach about 45cm (18in) and come in lots of different single colours. They are half-hardy, so sow under glass, or buy small plants.

Pot marigold (*Calendula*)

Another cottage garden favourite got at by the breeders! Perhaps the most authentic-looking variety still widely available is 'Indian Prince' which has very dark orange flowers on tall stems up to 50cm (20in) high.

Cornflower (*Centaurea cyanus*)

When a flower gives its name to a particular colour, it seems to me that that is what colour the flowers should be! So away with your pink, red, mauve and white versions and stick with cornflower blue. Probably the best variety is 'Blue Diadem'.

Sunflower (*Helianthus annuus*)

These are the real giants of cottage gardening, growing anything up to 9ft (3m) in height! There is now a much shorter-growing sunflower with a very large head, but it looks rather strange. Better to grow the old-fashioned 'Giant Single'; in the autumn dry the seeds and eat them – or feed them to the parrot.

Sweet pea (*Lathyrus odoratus*)

Although the Victorians bred many excellent varieties of sweet pea, the modern breeders have produced even more. For a cottage garden, go for those in soft colours and good perfume. You can grow them up pea sticks or, if you have hooped iron railings or a wooden picket fence, let them wend their way through that.

Night scented stock (*Matthiola bicornis*)

This hardy annual has small rather insignificant flowers, but its scent in the evening gives it its status. You could grow it with Virginian Stock (*Malcolmia maritima*), with much more attractive white, pink and mauve flowers but no perfume to speak of, to get the best of both worlds.

Ten week stock (*Matthiola incana*)

Grow these for their superb clove scent as well as their appearance. The seed is only available in mixed colours and needs to be sown under glass, but young plants are available from garden centres.

Tobacco plant (*Nicotiana*)

Although all tobacco plants have some scent the newer, multi-coloured hybrids have nothing like such a sweet perfume, especially in the evening, as the tall white *N. affinis*, so that's the one to go for.

Love-in-a-mist (*Nigella damascena*)

Another lovely cottage annual that's easily grown from seed. Although there is now a range of colours pink, mauve, white as well as the traditional cornflower blue, the latter is the best choice. 'Miss Jekyll' is still the best blue around.

Mignonette (*Reseda odorata*)

This is another annual with a wonderful scent, both day and night, though its small red and yellowish-green flowers are more curious than attractive.

Nasturtium (*Tropaeolum species*)

Happy in sun or light shade, and preferring a poor thin soil it is ideal for difficult places like the base of a hedge. And both leaves and flowers are also edible. Most of the modern hybrids like 'Whirlybird' and 'Gleam' are usually sold in mixtures but you can find single colours like 'Whirlybird Gold' and 'Gleam Scarlet'. Another stunning variety well worth tracking down is 'Empress of India' with smoky grey-green foliage and deep crimson flowers.

BULBS

Bulbs played an important role in the traditional cottage garden, and are equally valuable in the modern version because, given the right species, they can be part of the permanent planting. They come up every year to give their display and then, as their foliage dies down, it is concealed by the perennials starting into growth around them. The old-fashioned species bulbs are more authentic than the more garish modern hybrids. Many original cottagers would have taken bulbs from the wild so, with crocuses, for instance, go for something like the smaller, pastel coloured *C. chrysanthus* or *C. tomasinianus* rather than the big, bold, bright Dutch ones.

Ornamental onions (*Alliums*)

They range from the small *A. moly* which has clusters of butter-yellow flowers in June and the small rosy pink flowered *A. ostrowskianum* to the striking *A. christophii* which has heads of silvery-lilac flowers the size of grapefruit on stems 60 cm (2 ft) high.

Anemone

The starry blue or white flowers of *A. blanda* are lovely in March in a sunny or lightly shaded spot while, for planting in the moist shade under shrubs, the white flowered *A. nemorosa*, our native wood anemone, takes a lot of beating. When it is established, it forms a dense carpet of leaves but if it spreads too far, simply dig it up and divide it after it's finished flowering in late spring.

Crocus

There's a huge range on offer but for cottage gardens the smaller species of crocuses are your best bet. Among the chrysanthus hybrids look out for 'Blue Pearl', a delicate pale blue with a pearly sheen, 'Cream Beauty' and 'Snowbunting'. The very early flowering *C. tomasinianus*, with soft lilac flowers, is another good choice, or plant *C. ancyrensis* 'Golden Bunch', which can produce twenty flowers from one bulb, for a splash of gold.

Crown Imperial (*Fritillaria imperialis*)

This bulb is everything that, in theory, a cottage garden bulb shouldn't be. It is large, exotic and its crown of spiky green leaves on top of a cluster of large bell-like flowers makes it extremely showy. Yet it has been a great favourite in this country for more than four hundred years. Make sure you plant them deeply enough – with at least 15 cm (6 in) of soil on top – or they may not flower at all in the second year. If you have a heavy soil dig in plenty of grit before planting and plant the bulb on its side. That way water is less likely to penetrate, but the shoots will still come up the right way.

Snowdrops (*Galanthus nivalis*)

A common cottage garden bulb, the snowdrop is a welcome sight because it is the first sign that spring is in the air. The common snowdrop is delightful but for something a bit unusual try the double flowers *G.n.* 'Flore Pleno' or the much larger *G.n.* 'S Arnott'.

Lilies

Although lilies are very exotic-looking, some, like the Madonna or Cottage Lily (*Lilium candidum*), have been part of the cottage garden for centuries. They are well worth growing for their large sweetly scented trumpet flowers and are ideal in this situation because they dislike being disturbed; growing in among other plants they get the support they need without resorting to very *un*cottage-garden-like stakes!

They need a sharp well-drained soil (they did so well in the early cottage gardens because plenty of grit blew in from the unmade road. It is not particularly easy to get them established but it's well worth having a go. If you don't succeed try *L. regale* instead. The Turk's-cap lily (*L. martagon*) with its smaller reflexed pinky-purple flowers is another good choice. It does well in dappled shade and prefers a limey soil, but in a lime-free situation add some calcified seaweed to the soil when you're planting.

Daffodils (*Narcissus*)

Again in cottage gardens the smaller species are a better bet since they look better in a small space. The true wild daffodil *N. pseudonarcissus* is difficult to find in catalogues these days and of course taking them from the wild is illegal, but the similar Tenby daffodil (*N.p. obvallaris*) and *N. lobularis* with pale yellow and gold flowers are easier to find. Another very good small variety is the hoop petticoat daffodil (*N. bulbocodium*) with its rich butter-yellow flowers that look like, well, hooped petticoats, narrowing slightly at the end rather than flaring out in the usual trumpet shape. The *N. cyclamineus* hybrids are also a good choice, particularly in small gardens. Look for the small early-flowering 'Tête-à-Tête', the long-lasting 'Peeping Tom' and 'February Gold'.

Jonquils were also a great favourite for their wonderful perfume. Try *N. jonquilla* in a sheltered sunny spot, as close to the front door as you can find, so that you can enjoy the perfume as often as possible. The old pheasant's eye narcissus (*N. poeticus recurvus*) is another traditional favourite, with its white petals and orange red-rimmed eye, and it is one of the last to flower.

Tulip

Some of the species tulips are probably your best bet here. For one thing they are smaller and more in scale with small gardens, and less likely to get flattened by hurricane-force April showers. For another, they can be left in the soil year after year, unlike the tall garden tulips which need lifting and storing once they've finished flowering.

Look for *Tulipa tarda* whose butter-yellow flowers with a white edging open out almost flat, the lady tulip (*T. clusiana*) with slender white petals stained carmine on the outside and the Himalayan tulip (*T. chrysanthus*) with carmine outer petals and buttercup yellow inner ones. You could also try the water lily tulip (*T. kaufmanniana*) the petals of which have a creamy pink exterior and a white interior and which open almost flat in the sun. Some of the hybrids like 'Heart's Delight' are also worth trying.

Tulips were, and still are in a few places, 'florists' flowers'. The prized blooms have striped petals as a result of virus disease, and so are always grown separately. If you wanted to get a similar effect in mixed borders you could try a striped tulip like 'San Marino' or 'Sorbet' or even a parrot tulip like 'Flaming Parrot' or 'Estella Rijnveld'.

HERBS

In cottage gardens of the past, both perennial and annual herbs were much more than purely ornamental. Not only were they used in cooking where they added much needed flavour to a pretty bland diet and helped cover up the fact that any meat they were lucky enough to have might not be too fresh, but they were of great medicinal benefit, often being the only form of medication available for common ailments.

These days, although decorative herbs have their place, it's the culinary ones that are most valuable and besides, herbal medicine requires specialist knowledge: just because something grows in the garden doesn't mean it can't do you any harm.

Chives (*Allium schoenoprasum*)

The mildly onion-flavoured leaves are invaluable in cooking but with its clumps of tall slender leaves and clover-like pink flowers it also makes a very attractive edging plant for a path. It's a perennial but very easy to grow from seed initially. You could also try garlic chives for good garlic flavour and starry white flowers.

Dill (*Anethum graveolens*)

A valuable annual herb in that its leaves, flowers and seeds can all be used in cooking. It's also very attractive with its yellow flower heads and feathery foliage. It prefers a dry sunny spot well protected from the wind and will self-seed each year. Just pull it out if it becomes a nuisance.

Southernwood or Lad's Love (*Artemisia abrotanum*)

Many of the artemisias are superb silver foliage plants for a sunny border and although Southernwood is a medicinal herb, it's also a great beauty. (See page 32 for details.)

Borage (*Borago officinalis*)

This tall growing annual herb has blue-green hairy leaves and very pretty starry blue flowers all summer long. The flowers taste a bit like cucumber, and you can use them in salads as well as in drinks such as Pimms!

Chamomile (*Chamomilla recutita* and *nobilis*)

There are two types of chamomile, the German (*C. recutita*) which is an annual and perhaps better for chamomile tea and the Roman *C. nobilis* which is a perennial with a stronger, more bitter flavour. However it is a much better garden plant as it forms dense mats of ferny foliage, making it ideal for chamomile lawns. The best form for this purpose is the non-flowering *C. nobilis* 'Treneague', while for a border choose the double flowered *C.n.* 'Flore Pleno'.

Fennel (*Foeniculum vulgare*)

Another very attractive and useful herb, not dissimilar to dill in appearance, except that it grows to twice the height of just under 2m (6ft). In fact you shouldn't grow it too close to dill as they can cross-pollinate. Even more attractive than the green fennel is the bronze variety *F.v.* 'Purpureum' which has the same aniseed flavour and is, if anything, even hardier.

Lemon balm (*Melissa officinalis*)

The leaves of this herb have such a strong lemon scent they can be used instead of lemon rind in cooking. It also makes a refreshing tea. Even better than plain lemon balm are the golden and variegated kinds *M.o.* 'All Gold' and *M.o.* 'Aurea', which also do best in dappled shade.

Mint (*Mentha*)

Many members of this large family are well worth growing, from the common spearmint (*M. spicata*) and peppermint (*M. × piperita*), to the green and white variegated pineapple mint *M. suaveolens* 'Variegata' and pennyroyal (*M. pulegium*) used as a remedy for colds. Mint is extremely invasive, especially in the moist soils it prefers, and so should be contained in either a very large pot, an old sink or inside a bottomless bucket sunk into the soil. Make sure the bucket is proud of the soil though, otherwise the mint will simply spread on to the surrounding soil, rooting as it goes.

Marjoram (*Origanum*)

The perennial pot marjoram (*O. onites*) is the easiest to grow in a sunny spot but it has less flavour than the sweet marjoram (*O. marjorana*) or the perennial oregano (*O. vulgare*), neither of which are as reliably hardy. There is also a very attractive golden form *O. vulgare* 'Aureum'. While it needs sunlight to develop its full colour, it also needs protection from the midday sun, which can scorch the leaves, and so is happiest in dappled shade.

Parsley (*Petroselinum crispum*)

An essential cottage garden herb. You can grow it from seed as a biennial or an annual, although it has a reputation for being difficult to grow successfully. It's slow to germinate and must never dry out, so plenty of water and patience are the order of the day.

Rosemary (*Rosmarinus officinalis*)

This has been a feature of British gardens for centuries, although it needs a well-drained soil and a warm sheltered spot if it is to survive the winter. (As an insurance policy, stick a few sprigs in a pot of compost in late summer; they root very easily.) The common rosemary can reach 2 m (6 ft) in height and spread, so for small gardens choose *R.o.* 'Benenden Blue' or the even smaller *R.o.* 'Severn Sea', which grows to about 60 cm (2 ft).

Rue (*Ruta graveolens*)

This very attractive sub-shrub with its very attractive blue-green finely dissected leaves was grown for its medicinal, disinfectant and insecticidal (against fleas, in particular) properties. It is now grown mainly for its attractive foliage which is bluer and brighter when young, so cut the stems hard back in spring. Avoid handling it on a sunny day as it can cause painful blisters on the skin.

Sage (*Salvia officinalis*)

Another excellent medicinal and culinary herb, which likes well-drained soil and a sunny spot. Traditionally the cottage garden variety would have been the plain grey-green leafed one but you could stretch a point and grow the beautiful, though slightly less hardy, cream and pink variegated version, *S.o.* 'Tricolor'.

Thyme (*Thymus*)

This invaluable herb can be divided most usefully into two groups: creeping thymes (good varieties include 'Annie Hall', 'Bressingham Pink' and the variegated 'Doone Valley'); and upright ones (look for the lemon-scented *T. × citriodorus* and the variegated *T. vulgaris* 'Silver Posie'). While the creeping thymes have slightly less flavour, they are both valuable garden plants. They thrive at the front of a sunny border, or between paving slabs where they are likely to get trodden on occasionally; this releases their scent but does them no harm. You can also sow a thyme lawn, like the one at Sissinghurst where, on a warm summer's day, it's almost impossible to see the flowers for the blanket of bees!

FRUIT

The traditional cottage gardener certainly grew fruit in amongst the other border plants. Apples were popular – witness the venerable and gnarled old specimens that still exist today – while many gardens boasted plums, pears, cherries, and even, though more rarely, peaches. They were grown from pips or were the gift of enlightened landlords. In the 1820s John Claudius Loudon recommended saving valuable border space by growing fruit as cordons, espaliers or fans, against the cottage walls.

That remains good advice today and you can maximise space by growing them against post and wire supports to form a screen or even over metal arches to form an attractive, and productive, walkway. The use of dwarfing rootstocks means it is now possible to grow favourite varieties of fruit in the border without them taking up too much room.

Apples

Even in a small garden you ought to grow at least two different varieties so that they will pollinate each other. Or if you are on good terms with the neighbours, you could plant one in each garden. Choose either early flowering varieties like 'Discovery', 'Katy', 'Fiesta' and 'Kent' or late flowering ones such as 'Orleans Reinette', 'Ashmeads Kernel' and 'Suntan'. Don't choose one from each group or they won't pollinate very well. The best dwarfing rootstock here is M 106. It produces slightly larger trees than M 27, but the latter needs staking all its life and a very fertile soil to do well. Since your trees will be competing with other plants for nutrients and water, the M106 is a better bet.

Cherries

Even on a dwarfing rootstock like Colt they make pretty big trees, so they are best grown trained against a wall or fence. The only self-fertile sweet variety is 'Stella', although it doesn't have the best flavour. 'Morello', the acid cherry which is ideal for jam, is also self-fertile and is happy on a north-facing wall. It will pollinate sweet cherries that flower at the same time so if you have space for two, try 'Bigarreau Gaucher' as well.

Pears

Pears are more difficult to grow than apples. They are slower to come into fruit, hence the saying 'Plant pears for your heirs' – and they flower earlier so are more prone to frost damage. That problem can be overcome to some extent by growing them against a sheltered sunny wall or fence. Again, you should grow two to be sure that they pollinate each other. Choose either early flowering varieties like 'Conference', 'Williams' Bon Chrétien' or 'Beth' or, especially if you live in a frost-prone area, the late-flowering 'Onward' or 'Doyenné du Comice'.

Plums

The old Victoria plum tree is as much a feature of a traditional cottage garden as its apple equivalent – and as big! Now you can get Victoria plums grafted either on to a St Julien A rootstock, suitable for growing as a freestanding dwarf pyramid tree or as a fan, or on the smaller Pixy which can even be grown in pots. It's best to stick to a self-fertile variety and fortunately most of the good ones like 'Czar', 'Victoria' and 'Marjorie's Seedling' come into that category.

SOFT FRUIT

Blackcurrants

These are well worth growing for their fruit but they certainly don't justify a place in the garden for their looks alone. Grow them singly, surrounded by ornamental plants, which will not only compensate for their plainness but will also help ward off pests. Blackcurrants are particularly gross feeders, even when grown on their own with no competition from surrounding plants, so make sure you incorporate lots of manure when planting and give them two handfuls of blood, fish and bone in early spring. The best variety for small gardens is the new 'Ben Sarek' which is a good bit smaller than the older varieties but still crops well.

Gooseberries

You can grow them as bushes or if space is limited as single, double or triple cordons against a wall or fence. They can be grown as standards, on a bare stem, but they will need staking because when they are full of fruit the head can be very heavy indeed. Stakes look a bit out of place in the informality of a cottage garden but you can disguise most of the stake with the surrounding planting. New varieties which have good flavour and resistance to the dreaded gooseberry mildew include 'Jubilee' and 'Invicta'.

Grapes

In Victorian times many cottages, particularly in the south, were smothered in grape vines which grew up walls and over thatched roofs, not only producing grapes but looking very attractive too. According to records, at least a dozen named varieties flourished, some sweet, some for wine-making and some dual-purpose, some white, some red, some black. See pages 48–9 for suitable varieties.

Redcurrants

Oddly enough, these are more like gooseberries than blackcurrants and where space is at a premium they can be grown against a wall or fence as single, double or triple cordons. The best variety is 'Red Lake'.

Strawberries

These have featured in cottage gardens since the middle ages, transplanted from the wild. Thanks to the modern plant breeders' skill, by planting the right varieties you can have fruit from June until October. They are attractive, with their large clover-like leaves and white flowers, and look good planted in groups in a cottage garden border. Good varieties, in order of fruiting season, are 'Pantagruella', 'Idil', 'Elsanta', 'Hapil', 'Pandora' and 'Aromel'. At the front of the border, you could always try the exquisitely flavoured alpine strawberry.

VEGETABLES

The staple diet of everyone except the very rich, vegetables took pride of place in the original cottage garden. In the modern cottage garden, where vegetables don't need to be grown as a matter of economic necessity, it makes sense to choose just a few that are expensive to buy in the shops and which earn their keep for their appearance as well.

Artichokes

Globe artichokes are expensive to buy, and because their large, jagged blue-green leaves are attractive in their own right, you get double value from a crop that's home grown. Grow them from seed or buy 'suckers'. The best variety is still 'Green Globe'. Either grow them singly, dotted about in the middle of a border, or in groups of three.

Lettuce

There are now many different kinds to choose from, some of them very ornamental indeed. The cut-and-come-again lettuce 'Red Salad Bowl' is good value, the frilly-edged 'Lollo Rossa' and the small cos lettuce 'Little Gem'. Lamb's Lettuce or Corn Salad isn't really a lettuce at all, but makes an excellent salad crop for late summer and autumn that's expensive to buy but easy to grow. Sow it in the spring as you would ordinary lettuce and thin it out as necessary.

Marrows

These were another cottage garden favourite, though these days most of us eat them when young and small and tasty and call them courgettes. In an established cottage garden they probably take up too much space – a good square metre per plant – but in a new garden they are a valuable and productive space filler. Good varieties include 'Zucchini', 'Ambassador' and, for a bit of a splash, the golden-fruited 'Gold Rush'.

Runner beans

Another excellent cottage garden crop that offers attractive foliage, pretty flowers and lots of produce, as well as providing instant height in the garden. You can grow them up the traditional row of crossed canes or a wigwam of canes or strings, or they'll even climb up sloping canes fixed to the fence with wires. In a new garden, if you have put up an arch, you could grow them up that while waiting for your roses to get established. The old variety 'Painted Lady' is an excellent choice, with its mixture of red and white flowers, or you could achieve a similar effect by growing one red- and one white-flowered modern variety together. The stringless white-flowered 'Mergoles' and the red-flowered 'Red Knight' or 'Polestar' are good bets.

CHAPTER FOUR

The 1930s Semi Garden

*B*etween the wars thousands of large semis were built in leafy suburbs all over the country, many mock Tudor in style, brick-built with half-timbered gables and eaves. They were exactly the sort of houses that characterised 'Metroland', the housing estates that grew up in the 1920s and 1930s as the Metropolitan railway spread north-west of London through Middlesex, Hertfordshire and Bucking-hamshire.

They all had front gardens, of course, the style of which was broadly similar. A low brick or stone wall, depending on the locality, often with posts and black painted metal chains looped between them, a rectangular lawn bordered by narrow flowerbeds and perhaps geometrically shaped beds cut out of it, usually filled with spring bulbs and summer bedding. If there were roses, they would have been standards or hybrid teas.

There may well have been a single specimen tree such as an ornamental cherry or crab apple, a large conifer or a silver birch. As for ornamentation, you'd probably find a bird bath or a sundial set in the middle of the lawn.

This type of house was usually built for people of sufficient means to own a car (indeed the advertisements in the 1932 *Metroland* handbook assured would-be purchasers that 'you will not have a nasty cheap, mass production house anywhere near you to lower the value of your own property') and so many came with a garage attached and a drive neatly slicing the garden into two!

The keynote of these gardens and indeed the houses was neatness. The bedding would have been of uniform height and almost certainly planted in straight lines rather than in the drifts or clumps preferred today, and the edges of the lawn would have been always immaculately trimmed.

Our Suburban Semi Garden

Jenny and Bryan Pullinger's semi built in 1930 is very much in the Metroland mould, a solid house of soft red brick with half-timbered black and white gables and leaded windows. Their north-east-facing garden is also probably very much as it was when the house was built. As the garden is about 45 cm (18in) above the level of the pavement, there is a low retaining wall of 'stone' blocks set round the large rectangular lawn. At the entrance to the drive stands a beautiful multi-stemmed silver birch which, to guess from its size, must have been planted when the garden was first laid out.

When we first saw the garden, a small triangular bed to the left of the drive was dominated by a holly tree, whose lower branches were recently removed, partly to allow more light and moisture to penetrate what was a very dry shady area, and partly in response to the local authority's request to cut back all trees and shrubs overhanging the pavement. Bryan had tried to improve the area by putting in a few slabs of stone but, as he was the first to admit, not with any great success.

To the right of the drive, in the main part of the garden, the narrow borders surrounding the lawn were full of spring colour – bulbs and early-flowering alpines – and at first glance we wondered why Jenny and Bryan wanted a radical change.

But as we investigated further it became clear that once the bulbs had died down and the alpines had stopped flowering, there was practically nothing to take their place. In addition, the lawn, which had looked passable at a distance in March before the birch came into full leaf and took all the light, looked increasingly awful as the summer wore on, with bald patches that were baked hard and areas covered in moss or slime. None of the Pullingers' efforts over the years to revitalise the lawn with fertilisers, aeration or soil improvement had made the slightest difference.

Overall, it has to be said, the garden was rather dull. As keen gardeners (and indeed the back garden is a picture) the Pullingers were ashamed of their front garden and Jenny admitted that she always tried to whisk visitors through it as quickly as possible!

As well as being largely responsible for the problems with the lawn, the roots of the silver birch were beginning to push down parts of the retaining wall. But it was such a splendid tree that even if the Pullingers had been tempted to cut it down, they're quite certain that the other residents in their quiet cul-de-sac wouldn't have let them!

What they wanted was a garden they could be proud of all year round as well as a garden they could work in, since gardening gave them both a lot of pleasure. At the same time, they wanted something that would still be in keeping with the house and not wholly out of keeping with the other gardens in the road.

John Brookes, who is the best known British garden designer, felt that the best way to create a garden in sympathy with the house was not to look to the 1930s, but to look closely at the house itself for the scale for the garden and for the design ideas.

In his view, the original style of garden was all wrong for the type and size of house, something that had come about because the builders tried to pretend that their smart new homes were really grand country houses, just scaled down a bit. For a start, the large expanse of lawn was out of proportion to the house. John pointed out that the front elevation of the Pullingers' house could be broken down roughly into 12 ft squares. The bay window and the garage doors were about 12 ft square and, if you could have opened up the front, like a dolls' house, the rooms exposed would also be more or less the same size. But the lawn as it stood was more than twice that length and with the narrow borders, John felt that the garden looked like a living room with all the furniture pushed back against the walls, leaving a vast expanse of green, somewhat manky 'carpet' in the centre.

John decided to divide the front garden into smaller areas, more in proportion to the house itself. Looking at the house, he saw the striking effect of the stark, parallel lines of the black-stained wood against the white rendering and the triangular shape of the gable. He also saw exciting, less immediately obvious geometric shapes, like the semi-circular shape of the front step and of the paved area leading from the house on to the lawn. John decided to make the silver birch a feature of the garden, and to bring the retaining wall around it to make a bed, so curves and circles became the theme.

He also wanted to create a garden that looked good both from the street and from inside the house – one of the new small circular flowerbeds, for instance, was directly level with the front door – and also framed an attractive view of a church spire and mature trees in the middle-distance.

In the circular bed around the tree he put down gravel, since clearly grass would not thrive in such conditions, and planted it with shade-lovers and for winter colour, *Iris stylosa* and the architectural *Helleborus corsicus*, with apple-green flowers over leathery, spiky, mid-green leaves. At the front of the garden he created a large curved bed extending from the tree across the front of the garden and right down the boundary with the house next door, making a much wider border than previously.

John chose mainly foliage plants, many of them golden and some of them architectural, to add brightness to the rather shady conditions of this north-east-facing garden. These included evergreens like the golden yew, the golden privet, the shrubby honeysuckle (*Lonicera nitida* 'Baggesen's Gold') and the lovely little golden box-leafed holly (*Ilex crenata* 'Golden Gem'). He also selected some deciduous plants like the golden mock orange (*Philadelphus coronarius* 'Aureus') and the golden cut-leafed elder (*Sambucus racemosa* 'Plumosa Aurea'). The Pullingers had already begun to discover the merits of coloured foliage plants in the back garden and so were delighted with the choice.

The owner of this mock Tudor house, built in 1938, has created a garden
which is Tudor in feel, with formal shaped beds and topiary and which
marries perfectly with the house.

For some plain greens to set off the golds, John chose shade-tolerant hydrangeas like
H. villosa, which has large grey-green leaves with blue-lavender flower heads in late
summer/early autumn and attractive peeling bark in winter, and *H. arborescens*
'Annabelle' with huge, densely-packed white flower heads from summer through until
autumn. The only flower colour, apart from white hydrangeas and Japanese anemones,
was blue – in penstemons and the late-flowering *Ceratostigma willmottianum*, for
example, since blue and white look so good with gold.

When redesigning the centre of the garden, John removed the low double wall (using
the stone to extend the remaining wall around the tree) and replaced the remainder of the
lawn with an area of consolidated gravel planted with just a few clumps of spiky plants
like sisyrinchiums, the striped iris (*Iris pallida* 'Variegata') and the blue autumn-
flowering *Liriope muscari*. Here the Pullingers could also plant alpines and spring-
flowering bulbs which would give a pretty display before the birch took most of the light.

John planned to remove one of the square planters at the entrance to the garden, and
replace the stone semi-circle with a complete circle of crazy paving. In the central area,

John created two circular flowerbeds of different sizes, one with annuals of one colour – blue ageratums, or petunias, the other with golden sage and blue penstemons.

The house itself looked less welcoming than it might. John considered planting a climber to grow up the walls – an ivy or the climbing hydrangea, both of which would flourish on a north-east-facing wall. In the end he decided that it would eventually interfere with the architecture and so opted instead for two topiary balls of box planted in square black Versailles tubs. The real thing in wood would have cost too much, so instead we bought some good quality plastic ones and spray-painted them black.

To the left of the drive, John suggested removing the holly tree, rebuilt the wall in a more definite curve, and planted up the area with the same sorts of shrubs and perennials used in the main part of the garden. The Pullingers were thrilled with the finished garden, and so were the neighbours, who had been rather apprehensive about the changes initially. Many people noticed the beauty of the silver birch for the first time, and really felt the garden made a marvellous entrance to the rest of the close.

FOLIAGE PLANTS

Trees

Many of the small trees listed in Chapter 2 are grown for their attractive foliage, but particularly good are: the golden Indian bean tree (*Catalpa bignonioides* 'Aurea'); *Acer negundo* 'Flamingo'; *Gleditsia triacanthos*, either 'Elegantissima' or 'Sunburst'; *Robinia pseudoacacia*' 'Frisia'; the weeping willow-leafed pear (*Pyrus salicifolia* 'Pendula') and all the rowans (*Sorbus*) listed.

Climbers

There are some excellent climbing foliage plants listed in Chapter 3 including self-clingers like ivy, Virginia creeper and vine. The climbing hydrangea, although a flowering plant, deserves to be grown for its leaves alone.

Other good foliage climbers include:

Actinidia kolomikta

For a sunny wall, this is a very dramatic plant whose green leaves are splashed with white and pink. It will tolerate a bit of shade, but the colouring won't be as vivid as it is in full sun. It's a twining plant, so will need some sort of support.

Height: 4m (12ft).   **Sun**

Golden Hop (*Humulus lupulus* 'Aureus')

This rampant twining climber has fresh yellow leaves in spring and early summer which gradually fade to a lime green. Cut it back each spring for the brightest coloured new foliage.

Height: up to 6m (20ft).   **Sun**

SHRUBS

Japanese maples (*Acer palmatum*)
These are superb foliage shrubs. For details see page 25.
Part shade

Japanese Angelica Tree (*Aralia elata*)
For a sheltered garden with rich, moist not-too-alkaline soil this is a splendid specimen shrub, with huge pinnate olive green leaves up to 1.2m (4ft) long and 1m (3ft) wide. There are two variegated versions *A.e.* 'Variegata' with creamy-yellow variegations and the much brighter yellow and green *A.e.* 'Aureovariegata', which are very attractive but slightly less hardy than the plain one.
Height and spread after 10 years 3 × 2.5m (10 × 8ft).   Sun/very light shade

Tree of Heaven (*Ailanthus altissima*)
This fast-growing large tree produces the most spectacular foliage if grown as a shrub and cut back hard, almost to ground level, early each spring. Hacking any tree back so hard and so regularly will obviously weaken it eventually so feed it well and be prepared to replace it every few years.
Height (in one season): 2.4m (8ft),   Sun/light shade

Spotted laurel (*Aucuba japonica*)
This is a valuable shrub in a dry shady spot because it will at least grow and give a splash of colour where little else will. Given a bit more light and moisture, it can be a very handsome shrub indeed, particularly if you choose *A.j.* 'Crotonifolia', which has speckled rather than more boldly variegated green and gold leaves.
Height and spread after 10 years: 1.8 × 1.8m (5ft 6in × 5ft 6in).   Sun/part shade/shade

Berberis
This family of evergreen and deciduous shrubs is grown mainly for its foliage. There are many cultivars of *B. thunbergii* which have lovely coloured foliage: bright yellow (*B.t.* 'Aurea'); wine red (*B.t.* 'Bagatelle', 'Helmond Pillar' and 'Red Pillar'); or even the mottled wine red and pink foliage of *B.t.* 'Harlequin'.

Elaeagnus
The best deciduous variety is *E. commutata* (or *E. argentea*) which has attractive silver foliage. The two most widely grown evergreen members of the family, *E.* × *ebbingei* and *E. pungens*, are prized for their variegated forms, *E.* × *e.* 'Gilt Edge', the leaves of which have pale yellow margins, and *E. pungens* 'Maculata' whose leaves have central bright gold splashes and which will lighten up a shady corner as nothing else can. Its new

growth is such an extraordinary shade of metallic bronze that you'd be forgiven for thinking someone has been playing tricks with an aerosol of paint. Its only vices are quite vicious thorns and a tendency to revert to plain green. As soon as you spot any plain green growths, cut them out.

Height and spread after 10 years: 2 × 2 m (6 × 6 ft). Sun/part shade/shade

Euonymus fortunei

A valuable shrub for sun or shade. See page 112.

Fatshedera lizei

A cross between fatsia and ivy, its leaves reveal its parentage very clearly! It is an excellent lax-growing foliage shrub for a very shady corner or to be trained against a shady wall.

Height and spread after ten years: 1.2 × 4 m (4 × 13 ft). Part shade/shade

False caster oil plant (*Fatsia japonica*)

Another excellent architectural evergreen foliage shrub. See page 112.

Hebe

Another excellent family of flowering shrubs many of whose members such as *H. pinguifolia* 'Pagei', *H. albicans* and *H.a.* 'Red Edge', plus the variegated *H.* × *franciscana* 'Variegata' are worth growing for their foliage alone. See page 112.

Holly (*Ilex*)

This marvellous family of evergreen foliage shrubs has something to suit every situation. Among the best of the larger-growing varieties are the plain *I. aquiuifolium* 'J.C. van Tol', the silver variegated *I.a.* 'Silver Queen', and the golden variegated *I.* × *altaclarensis* 'Golden King'. Among the smaller kinds, the hedgehog holly (*I. aquifolium* 'Ferox') is excellent, particularly the silver and golden variegated forms (*I.a.* 'Ferox Argentea' and 'Aurea' respectively) as is the very low-growing box leafed holly *I. crenata*. Its variegated form and the gold-leafed *I.c.* 'Golden Gem' are excellent, although the latter needs a degree of shade to prevent scorching of its leaves, but not too much shade or the glorious golden colour fades to a less interesting yellow-green.

Height and spread after 10 years: 60 cm − 4 m × 1 – 2.5 m (2 − 13 × 3 − 8 ft). Sun/part shade/shade

Privet (*Ligustrum ovalifolium*)

A semi-evergreen shrub whose image has been dented by its use as suburban hedging and its propensity to suck all the nutrients and moisture out of the surrounding soil. However, it can be very useful in dryish soils and shade where not much else will grow.

Height and spread after 10 years: 4 × 4 m (13 × 13 ft) if left unclipped. Part shade/shade

Mahonia

Another excellent evergreen architectural shrub with its whorls of long, jagged, leathery leaves, some of which take on a red or purple tint in winter. The scented yellow flowers in winter are a bonus. The small *M. aquifolium* is a good ground coverer and responds well to cutting back hard every three or four years. Of the larger mahonias *M.a.* 'Apollo', *M.* × 'Charity' and *M. japonica* are all good and widely available. *M. lomariifolia* and *M. undulata* (with wavy leaves) are excellent too, but harder to come by.

Height and spread after 10 years: 1 – 3 × 2 – 2.8 m (3 – 10 × 6 – 9 ft).   Sun/part shade/shade

Paulownia tomentosa

Another tree which produces huge and spectacular leaves if it's grown as a shrub and cut back hard each spring, although that way you lose any chance of the foxglove-like flowers which give it one of its common names.

Height in one season: 2 m (6 ft).   Sun/light shade

Pieris

A first class foliage shrub for an acid soil. See page 113.

Pittosporum

Much loved by flower arrangers, this family of foliage shrubs is less widely grown than it should be because people often assume it's not as hardy as it is. *P. tenuifolium* has small shiny olive green foliage with slightly wavy edges and black stems. *P.t.* 'Garnettii' is probably the hardiest of the variegated forms, with pale grey-green leaves edged in white which flush pink in cold weather. The Japanese *P. tobira* is more tender and will only succeed outside in a warm sheltered spot.

Height and spread after 10 years: 3 × 2 m (10 × 6 ft).   Sun/very light shade

Rosa glauca (rubrifolia)

Probably the only rose worth growing for its foliage alone, this one has wonderful smoky bluey-mauve foliage. The single pink flowers in June and the small red heps in autumn are bonuses.

Height and spread after 10 years: 2 × 2 m (6 × 6 ft).   Sun

Rubus

Ornamental relatives of the bramble grown for their foliage and stems. Among the best for ground cover are the evergreen *R. calycinoides*, which forms an almost flat dense mat of puckered, dark green three- or five-lobed leaves, and the larger *R. tricolor*, whose green leaves are tinged red with white undersides (hence its name) and which is excellent in dry shade under trees, spreading up to 3 m (10 ft).

Height and spread after 10 years: 5 – 50 cm × 1 – 3 m (2 – 18 in × 3 – 10 ft).
Part shade/shade. Will tolerate sun.

Salix

Among the best small foliage shrubs are the low-growing *S. helvetica* with small pointed silvery leaves and white undersides, the creeping *S. repens* 'Argentea' and *S. lanata*, with woolly silver leaves. The taller coyote willow (*S. exigua*) has beautiful delicate silver foliage and responds well to cutting back hard every year or two.

Height and spread: 1–3 × 1.5–3 m (1–10 × 5–10 ft).   Sun/part shade

Golden cut-leafed elder (*Sambucus racemosa* 'Plumosa Aurea')

The best foliage is produced on young growth so cut it back hard in spring. If you want some flowers and berries then cut back between half and a third of the stems.

Height in one season 1.2 × 1.2 m (4 × 4 ft).   Dappled shade

Senecio 'Sunshine'

So many lovely silver foliage shrubs like this bear unattractive, acid-yellow flowers, so snip off the buds to encourage the plant to produce new silver foliage instead. It needs cutting back hard regularly. Botanists have recently renamed this *Brachyglottis* 'Sunshine'.

Height and spread: 1 × 1 m (3 × 3 ft).   Sun/very light shade

Viburnum

The best small viburnum for foliage is *V. davidii* (see page 115) but for larger gardens the large and stately *V. rhytidophyllum* is hard to beat. It has long, large, deeply wrinkled leaves with brown felty undersides. It does flower but these are insignificant and a rather grubby white. But its berries, first red then turning black, are a bonus.

Height and spread: 3 × 3 m (10 × 10 ft).   Part shade/shade. Tolerates sun.

Yucca

These bring a touch of the exotic to almost any garden, for they are tougher than they look and can stand up to −10°C. Good varieties include *Y. filamentosa*, whose leaves carry small curly white threads, *Y. flaccida*, *Y. gloriosa*, tinged red, and *Y. recurvata*, which also has a subtle variegated form. The spikes of all yuccas are very sharp so it's not a plant for a garden used by small children.

Height and spread: 2 × 2 m (6 × 6 ft).   Sun

HERBACEOUS FOLIAGE PLANTS

Bear's Breeches (*Acanthus spinosus*)

This sports tall spikes of strange hooded mauve and white flowers in mid-summer, but it is worth having for its jagged foliage alone. There is an even more deeply divided variety *A. spinosissimus* which is positively skeletal.

Height: 1.2 m (4 ft).   Sun

Bugle *(Ajuga reptans)*
An invaluable carpeter with very attractive coloured foliage. See page 150.
Sun/part shade

Lady's mantle *(Alchemilla mollis)*
Another flowering perennial that's worth having for its foliage alone, in this case pale green beautiful folded fan-like leaves. See page 52.

Ballota pseudodictamnus
Ideal for a very dry sunny spot, sending out long stems clothed in small round felt-like silver leaves.
Height: 75 cm (2 ft 6 in).   Sun

Elephant's ears *(Bergenia)*
The solid round leathery evergreen leaves are very useful as a contrast to more ornate or spiky foliage. See page 152.
Sun/shade

Cardoon *(Cynara cardunculus)*
Although this was once a popular vegetable, it is now grown mainly for its huge dramatic jagged grey-green leaves. You can grow its close relative the globe artichoke (*C. scolymus*) which has equally good leaves but cutting the produce to eat will rather spoil the look of the plant.
Height: 2 m (6 ft).   Sun

Sea holly *(Eryngium)*
These spiky plants, much-loved by flower arrangers, are grown as much for their silver foliage as their curious greenish-silver or blue flowers. The tallest variety is *E. agavifolium* which grows to over 1.5 m (5 ft) in height, but well worth growing are Miss Willmott's Ghost (*E. giganteum*), so called because the famous Victorian gardener Miss Willmott was supposed to have scattered its seed in every garden she visited, and the dramatic *E. × oliverianum* which has jagged green leaves but stems, bracts and flowers in a startling metallic blue.
Height: 75 cm (2 ft).   Sun

Spurge *(Euphorbia)*
Many members of this family are superb architectural foliage plants. In addition to those on page 152, *E. characias wulfenii* which has tall stems clothed in spiky blue grey foliage and huge heads of lime green bracts in May is excellent for a dry, sunny spot.
Height: 1.2 m (4 ft).   Sun

Filipendula ulmaria 'Aurea'

A superb golden foliage plant for moist soil in dappled shade. It does have flowers but they are insignificant so snip them off and get fresh new leaves.

Height: 45 cm (1 ft 6 in).   Part shade.

Fuchsia magellanica 'Gracilis' or 'Versicolor'

One of the hardy fuchsias, it has small vivid red flowers in late summer but they are less interesting than the cream, green and pink variegated foliage. The frost will cut it back to ground level in most winters but if not, cut it back hard in late spring.

Height: 60 cm (2 ft).   Sun/part shade

Hosta

A superb family of foliage plants, provided you can solve the slug problem. See pages 153–4.

Part shade/shade

Houttuynia cordata 'Chamaeleon'

With its green, cream and red foliage it makes very attractive ground cover in moist soil and dappled shade.

Height: 10 cm (4 in).   Part shade

Iris pallida 'Variegata'

This tall, spiky, pale green and cream iris is an excellent contrast in leaf shape to round foliage plants like bergenias. It also has blue flowers in June/July.

Height: 60 cm (2 ft).   Sun

Creeping Jenny (*Lysimachia nummularia* 'Aurea')

Another very good, ground-cover foliage plant with small round yellow leaves and bright yellow flowers in summer. Best grown in moist soil.

Height: 5 cm (2 in).   Sun/part shade

Plume poppy (*Macleaya cordata*)

Although it has towering (up to 1.5 m (5 ft) tall) spikes of tiny buff-coloured flowers in late summer, it's worth having primarily for its large beautifully lobed grey-green leaves with silvery-white undersides. It seeds itself with abandon.

New Zealand flax (*Phormium*)

These tall spiky plants are excellent, though some are more tender than others. *P. cookianum* and its hybrids seem hardier than some of the *P. tenax* hybrids. However *P.t.* 'Purpureum', with deep purplish leaves, and *P.t.* 'Bronze Baby', 'Sundowner'

The smooth, round shape of the clipped golden privet framing the front door,
is a perfect foil for the large, glossy, mid-green hand-shaped leaves of the
Fatsia japonica.

and 'Maori Sunrise' – all in shades of bronze, wine red and pink – plus the green-edged yellow 'Yellow Wave' are all worth trying in a sheltered sunny garden or in containers where they can be given winter protection in an unheated porch or greenhouse.

Height: 1.5m (5ft). Sun

Ornamental rhubarb (*Rheum palmatum*)

One of the most striking foliage plants whose large leaves are much more jagged than its edible relatives'. *R.p.* 'Atrosanguineum' has red tinged leaves when young which turn green on the top but keep the red colour underneath. It has plumes of fluffy crimson flowers in early summer. For small gardens *R.* 'Ace of Hearts' which only reaches about two thirds the size is a better bet. They must have rich, moist soil, to thrive.

Height: 1.2–2m (4–6ft). Sun

Caster oil plant (*Ricinus communis*)

In tropical climates this foliage plant with dramatic large bronze leaves is an evergreen shrub but in our climate it's best grown from seed as an annual – look for *R.c.* 'Impala'. It needs a sunny spot and rich soil. The seeds are poisonous.
Height: 1 m (3 ft 3 in).

Rodgersia

A superb plant with large, handsome leaves similar to but smaller than the Rheum family. It does best in a sunny spot in very moist or even wet soil, though it will also grow in shade provided the soil is damp and never dries out. Good varieties include *R. podophylla* whose leaves unfurl bronze, turn mid-green and later become copper and *R. pinnata* 'Superba' which has similar but darker leaves.
Height: 1–1.2 m (3–4 ft).   Sun/part shade

Rue (*Ruta graveolens* 'Jackman's Blue')

A valuable foliage plant for its rounded lacy leaves in blue. Cut back hard each spring for the brightest colour. Its sap can cause a painful skin allergy when exposed to sunlight so always wear rubber gloves when handling it.
Height: 60 cm (2 ft).   Sun

Lamb's lugs (*Stachys lanata* or *olympica*)

Another excellent silver foliage plant, especially the non-flowering 'Silver Carpet'. See page 156.

GRASSES

These are such excellent, if somewhat neglected, foliage plants that they deserve a section to themselves. As they are becoming more popular you will find a few varieties in garden centres but for a wide selection you may well have to buy mail order from a specialist such as P.W. Plants in Kenninghall, Norfolk or Beth Chatto in Elmstead Market near Colchester.

Bamboo (*Arundinaria*)

Some varieties are excellent foliage plants, which not only look good all year round, but add the unexpected dimension of sound to the garden as the breeze ruffles the leaves. Good varieties for small gardens include the dwarf golden variegated *A. viridistriata* which gives its best colour in full sun, providing you cut the old canes to ground level in spring. Or try the more subtle green and white striped *A. variegata*. Good taller varieties which are non-invasive include *A. nitida* and the graceful arching *A. murielae* which will

reach 3 m (10 ft) or more in a sunny spot though less in a shady spot.
Height: 75 cm–3 m (2–10 ft). Sun/part shade

Hakonechloa macra 'Albo-aurea'
The only problem with this grass which has vividly variegated leaves is that it is so attractive that stockists are always running out of it! It tolerates dry-ish soil and is excellent in a pot.
Height: 40 cm (16 in). Sun

Blue oat grass (*Helictotrichon* or *Avena sempervirens*)
This has vivid blue-grey evergreen leaves with plumes of tiny flowers much the same colour. *H.s.* 'Sapphire Spray' has even more vivid foliage. Both are happy in dry soil.
Height: 1.2 m (4 ft). Sun

Holcus mollis 'Variegatus'
The white stripes on the leaves are so broad that in spring it can look like an all-white carpet. It can be invasive but responds easily to a deftly wielded spade!
Height: 15 cm (6 in). Sun/shade

Woodrush (*Luzula maxima* 'Marginata')
Excellent for ground cover, especially where the soil is moist, though it gives a pretty good account of itself in dry soil too. Its rich green leaves are striped with white. In summer it has drooping sprays of tiny golden brown flowers.
Height: 45 cm (18 in). Sun/shade

Sedge (*Carex*)
Sedges are excellent for damp soils and look wonderful near ponds. *C. morrowii* 'Evergold' has slim bright gold leaves with green margins erupting from the centre of each clump, while the taller *C. stricta* 'Bowles Golden' has lovely bright gold foliage.
Height: 25–60 cm (10 in – 2 ft). Sun

Tufted hair grass (*Deschampsia caespitosa*)
Despite its foreign-sounding botanical name, this is one of our native grasses and one of the most beautiful too. It bears narrow arching leaves and its tall plumes of tiny silvery flowers look just as attractive in winter after they have died! Look for *D.c.* 'Gold Veil' or 'Bronze Veil' or the newer 'Golden Dew' with much shorter flower spikes.
Height: 75 cm – 1.3 m (2 ft 6 in – 4 ft). Sun/part shade

Festuca glauca 'Silver Sea'
The bluest of the blue grasses, this makes neat clumps in any sunny dry spot.
Height: 25 cm (10 in). Sun

Before (*right*) and after (*below* and *left*)

The clean, geometric lines of our 1930s semi garden stand out very clearly, although the planting is already beginning to soften them. The new wall round the existing silver birch makes a real feature of it.

Glyceria maxima 'Variegata'

Good in damp heavy soil, the broad green, yellow and white strap-like leaves of this grass are tinged pink in winter.

Height: 60cm (2ft).   Sun

Bowles golden grass *(Milium effusum 'Aureum')*

This evergreen grass provides a splash of sunlight in any shady spot, particularly in winter. Beth Chatto grows it with the purple leafed *Viola labradorica* and snowdrops.

Height: 40cm (16in).   Part shade/shade

Miscanthus

Another excellent family of tall elegant grasses with some very attractive variegated forms. Among the best plain ones are *M. sinensis* 'Gracillimus' with very dark green narrow leaves and *M.s.* 'Silver Feather', so called because of its silvery plumes, up to 2.4m (8ft) tall. Of the variegated kinds try *M.s.* 'Variegatus' or the unusual horizontally striped *M.s.* 'Zebrinus' with gold bands across its dark green leaves. They all look particularly good in gravel.

Height: 1.2 – 2m (4 – 6ft).   Sun

Molinia caerulea 'Variegata'

A beautiful neat little grass with subtle cream and green variegated leaves which turn a warm buff colour, together with its plumes of flowers, in autumn.

Height: 45cm (18in).   Sun

Gardeners' garters *(Phalaris arundinacea 'Picta')*

In a moist soil and a shady spot, this cool green and white grass looks very good indeed. Unfortunately it is invasive so either chop it back regularly or grow it in a confined space.

Height: 1m (3ft).   Part shade

Sasa veitchii

A bamboo that doesn't look like one at all, with tough, broad, paddle-like leaves whose edges become bleached as the summer wears on, giving a variegated effect. It is pretty rampant, so is best used in large gardens or where its wanderings can be confined.

Height: 1.2m (4ft).   Sun

Golden oats *(Stipa gigantea)*

An excellent evergreen grass for bringing instant height to a newly planted border since its plumes of oats, more silvery than golden, reach 2.5m (8ft) or more. Like those of other grasses, they remain attractive in winter once they have died, especially when rimed with frost.

Height: 2.5m (8ft).   Sun

FERNS

Given their natural woodland habitat, almost all ferns like shade and a moist soil. Again, while you will find some in garden centres, you may have to buy anything out of the ordinary through mail order from a fern specialist such as J. and D. Marston in Driffield, East Yorkshire or Fibrex in Stratford upon Avon.

Hardy maidenhair fern (*Adiantum* and *Asplenium*)
These small ferns are ideal in a partly shaded spot in acid soil where it's not too dry. Look for *A. pedatum*, the smaller *A.p.* 'Minor' and the carpeting *A. venustum*. If you can find them, the maidenhair and black spleenworts (*Asplenium trichomanes* and *A. adiantum-nigrum*) will add instant age to a wall or steps.
Height: 15 – 20 cm (6 – 8 in).

Lady fern (*Athyrium filix-femina*)
This native fern is no less attractive for being common. The smaller *A.f-f.* 'Minutum' is, as its name suggests, a miniature version, reaching only about 12 cm (5 in).
Height: 60 cm – 1.2 m (2 – 4 ft).

Male fern (*Dryopteris filix-mas*)
Another excellent and easy fern for deep shade. In mild areas it can keep its fronds through the winter, through which new bright green ones unfurl in spring.
Height: 1 m (3 ft).

Shuttlecock or ostrich plume fern (*Matteuccia struthiopteris*)
One of the most beautiful of all ferns, this has the most delicate divided fronds arranged just like the flights on a shuttlecock. It needs really damp soil to do well.
Height: 1 m (3 ft).

***Polypodium vulgare* 'Cornubiense'**
A small lacy evergreen fern, this one is particularly useful because it will put up with slightly drier soil than most other ferns.
Height: 30 cm (1 ft).

Soft shield fern (*Polystichum setiferum*)
Perhaps the most finely divided of all ferns, this evergreen or semi-evergreen fern will also tolerate slightly drier soil, though it is lusher and greener where the soil is moist. There are a number of varieties available, divided into two main groups, the *P.s.* 'Acutilobum' whose leaves are tough and sharp in outline and 'Divisilobum' which has softer leaves and is fuzzier in outline.
Height: 60 cm (2 ft).

CHAPTER FIVE

THE LOW-MAINTENANCE GARDEN

*F*or many people, the ideal front garden is one that looks good all year round but doesn't require a great deal of maintenance. Young couples who are both working and have active social lives have hardly enough time to spend on their back garden, never mind the front. Couples with young children are also short on time: their concern is for a front garden that looks tidy and has safe boundaries so that the children can't escape onto the road. And while older people may have both the time and inclination for gardening, they may not have the energy or the physical strength to do much more than potter. For all these groups, a low-maintenance front garden is the ideal solution.

Planning such a garden means identifying the repetitive, routine work and reducing it to the bare minimum. Lawns, for example, are high maintenance, especially if beds are cut out of the lawn; not only is mowing at least once a week a fiddly job (and awkward, too, if you live in a terrace when the mower has to be carted through the house) but trimming the edges, feeding, watering, scarifying and so on all take up a lot of time. So in a low-maintenance garden the lawn will go, and be replaced with a labour-saving and more attractive alternative – a mixture of hard landscaping, and ground-cover plants.

Formal hedges also need a lot of looking after, especially shrubs like privet which need trimming two or three times a year. Most conifer hedges don't need trimming quite so often, but keeping something like the rapidly-growing Leyland Cypress (*Cupressocyparis leylandii*) within reasonable bounds is a major undertaking. Informal hedges, usually consisting of evergreen flowering and berrying shrubs like firethorn (*Pyracantha*) and *Viburnum tinus*, only need an annual trim, and sometimes not even that.

Annuals are high-maintenance, too. Even if you buy them from the garden centre they need planting out, and then watering and dead-heading regularly if they are to go on flowering throughout the summer months. Much better to invest in easy-care ground cover plants which largely look after themselves. Hybrid tea and floribunda roses need a lot of work: pruning at least once a year, feeding and probably spraying against greenfly, blackspot, mildew and rust. Instead go for shrub roses, old or modern, or patio roses, which don't need regular pruning and, if you choose the right varieties, are more disease-resistant, too.

But, of course, it all depends on what you, personally, mean by 'work'. Something that gives you pleasure isn't a chore and if you enjoy wandering round the garden dead-heading as you go, or even mowing (and believe it or not some people do!) then by all means grow as many annuals or as much lawn as you like.

Our Low-Maintenance Garden

The plot we chose to transform into a low-maintenance front garden was already, indisputably, low-maintenance. What *was* in dispute, though, was whether or not you could legitimately describe it as a 'garden'! Previous owners had paved the entire area from boundary to boundary and from street to front door with custard-coloured, concrete paving slabs. The only trace of plant life were the few pathetic weeds which struggled up through the gaps between them. There wasn't even a front wall or hedges between it and the neighbours to help break it up a bit!

The house, a fairly standard early 1960s brick semi with an integral garage, didn't have a great deal to recommend it architecturally. The front door had virtually disappeared behind sliding patio doors and looked more like a large window than anything. And certainly, the bleakness of the garden made the house seem even more cold and unwelcoming.

Its owner, Beryl Whitten, who is seventy years old, moved there two years ago with her son Andrew. She had always enjoyed gardening, and what made her buy the property, despite the depressing first impressions, were the house itself, the quiet location and the terraced back garden.

She had made the back garden very pretty and used the small greenhouse in the far corner for raising annuals from seed to fill out the borders and to plant up hanging baskets and containers in a brave attempt to cheer up the front garden. It faces south and so they dry out very quickly in warm weather. During our last hot summer, Beryl found she was climbing on to a stool sometimes twice a day to water the hanging baskets outside the front door – not to be recommended for someone with arthritic hands and who has also undergone major surgery recently. But, despite all her valiant efforts, the front garden still looked very depressing, from both inside and outside the house.

What Beryl wanted was a garden to be proud of, a garden to enjoy pottering in and, since her son Andrew had enough to do keeping the back garden tidy, a garden that needed only minimum maintenance. We invited leading garden designer Robin Williams to come up with a plan for her garden. As the man responsible for the medal-winning Help the Aged gardens at the Chelsea Flower Show for the past seven years, he understands only too well the needs of elderly gardeners.

Robin's philosophy on front gardens is simple – they should be a frame for the house and should say 'Welcome'. Beryl's clearly did neither. His first thought was that since the one thing about any house that you can't change (at least not without a lot of effort and expense) is the colour of the bricks, the hard landscaping of the front garden and the planting should tone in with those. That meant the custard-coloured slabs, which clashed horribly with the soft orange-red of the bricks, would have to go.

Robin was relieved that the bricks were that warm, mellow colour, because the range of plants that would look good against it is much wider than for blue-red bricks. And he would paint the different coloured windowsills, garage doors and guttering all the same shade. He also wanted to make much more of the front door.

Although he had to cater for a car, Robin's overall plan was to create a garden that looked like a garden first and foremost, and not a car park when the car wasn't there. The fact that it had to accommodate a driveway meant the 'bones' of the garden had to be formal rather than informal, though he planned to make the planting very soft and informal. He also wanted to create a garden that looked good from two angles – from the front-room windows and from the street.

The garden also sloped, and although it seemed very gentle, the drop was in fact 75 cm (2 ft 6 in) from house to pavement – something else to be taken into account in the design.

Low-maintenance gardens, particularly for the elderly or for people with disabilities, usually involve raised beds so that people can garden at waist height, from a wheelchair or while sitting on a stool or, if they are standing up, without having to bend. But Robin isn't convinced that this is always the best solution because unless the beds are very narrow, it can be quite awkward to use tools horizontally. He believes it's often better to create a low-maintenance garden at ground level, with easy-care ground cover plants. What work that needs doing initially – the odd bit of hoeing perhaps – can be done with long-handled tools used vertically.

For Beryl's garden, Robin created a sort-of raised bed and, to cope with the slope, he designed a retaining wall, just over 60 cm (2 ft) high, parallel with the front boundary and curving back into the garden to delineate one side of the drive. The wall stays level, but since the garden slopes up to the house, it actually reduces gradually in height to 10 cm (4 in) – one brick's depth. The resulting planting area meant that Beryl could either potter around the wall at pavement level and garden at waist-height, or walk into it from the front door, and use long-handled tools. It also means that the view from the front windows is very pretty and at the same time passers-by get an attractive view of the garden too.

For the drive itself Robin chose a large diamond pattern picked out in the same bricks as the house, infilled with soft buff Rialta setts laid in a fish scale pattern. Beyond the retaining wall, the drive opens out to pass right across the front door, allowing plenty of space for driver and passengers to get out of the car.

To make more of the front door Robin created a step with a pitched roofed porch over it, tiled to match the tiles on the front bay, and with climbing plants around it. Since the house faces south there was a vast range to choose from but, as Beryl loves roses, he suggested 'Golden Showers' – a good choice because it has masses of yellow blooms all summer and because it won't grow too large, Beryl won't have to climb steps to tie it in or to prune it!

Boundaries did present a slight problem, since the rest of the estate was largely open plan, with a restriction that's still enforced by the local council on any boundary over 75 cm (2 ft 6 in) high. Robin wasn't in favour of a low wall around the garden anyway – it would just be a magnet for all the local dogs – so instead he opted for a low hedge of catmint (*Nepeta mussinii*), which would thrive in the hot dry conditions, in front of the retaining wall and a lavender hedge along the boundary between Beryl's garden and her neighbours to the west.

As for the rest of the planting, Robin chose similar, tough, drought-loving evergreens with steel-blue or gold foliage and long-lasting perennials with flowers in warm oranges and golds (colours that Beryl loves) with just a touch of blue here and there, like more lavender or the *Hebe* 'Marjorie'.

Beryl was also very keen to have a tree and Robin thought there might be room for two, one in the south-east corner – a small maple – *Acer henryi* – and another narrow growing tree on the far side of the garage doors, to help frame the house. Robin thought an upright, slow-growing conifer like *Thuja orientalis* 'Conspicua' would be ideal.

Although Beryl would have loved a Japanese maple, Robin pointed out it would not have survived in those hot, dry exposed conditions. They need protection from the overhead sun or their delicate foliage just shrivels and dies. Instead he suggested something like *Physocarpus opulifolius* 'Dart's Gold', a deciduous golden foliage shrub which has similar shaped leaves to the acer but would cope with those conditions much better. As he says, designing a garden is about deciding what you would like, then seeing what is feasible and, if needs be, thinking laterally to find suitable alternatives.

Sculpture: Alexander Relph

The very successful combination of paving and evergreen foliage plants chosen for contrast
in colour, shape and texture make this garden easy to maintain and attractive to look
at all year round.

Beryl was absolutely delighted with her garden. She particularly loved the pale yellow
Coreopsis verticillata 'Moonbeam', planted by three large boulders, and was already
thinking about plants she might add next year.

THE PRINCIPLES OF LOW-MAINTENANCE GARDENING

If you want to make an existing front garden into a low-maintenance garden, then the
first thing to do is identify the areas that are currently high maintenance and see how the
work can be reduced. Lawns are one of the major culprits here, and all too often the end
result simply doesn't repay the amount of time and effort invested in them. Small patches
of grass rarely look good – and most front gardens only have small patches of grass. They
often suffer from the shade cast by trees either in the garden itself or in the neighbour's
garden, or indeed from trees in the street. Lawns may be starved not only of light, but of
moisture and nutrients by greedy hedges growing nearby – another reason why they
often look thin and patchy.

So ask yourself, do you really need a lawn? In a back garden, its functions are primarily practical, providing somewhere to put the deck chairs, for the children to play, and to stretch out and sunbathe; but very few of us use our front gardens in those ways. Its decorative function is to set off the borders to their best advantage, and while it's true that there's nothing like a good-looking, well-kept lawn for doing that, most front garden lawns don't come into that category.

Many people cling on to their patch of scrubby lawn, I suspect, because they think that the only alternative is concrete or tarmac. But nothing could be further from the truth and there is, fortunately, a happy medium: a combination of hard surfaces for ease of maintenance and of soft planting with a range of shrubs and perennials chosen for their ability to look after themselves.

Instead of a small patch of grass, imagine attractive stone paving, real or imitation, enclosing a square, circle or diamond shape of low-growing, carpet-forming thyme. It's evergreen, covered in tiny pink, mauve or white flowers in the summer, it suppresses all weeds and it doesn't need mowing (just trimming back round the edges once a year or so when it gets ideas beyond its station). There's also a very low growing Corsican mint (*Mentha requienii*) which doesn't reach much more than 1 cm (½ in) in height. Its tiny, bright green leaves have the most wonderful mint smell when crushed, and it is covered in purple flowers, slightly bigger than a pinhead, in summer. Or what about a chamomile lawn, another evergreen scented herb with fern-like bright green leaves which doesn't reach more than about 10 cm (4 in) in height and again only needs trimming back when it outgrows its allotted space? An unusual alternative would be sea thrift (*Armeria maritima*), which has narrow, grass-like deep green leaves about 20 cm (4 in) high and, depending on the variety, white or pink flowers for a long period in the summer. It forms slightly rounded clumps rather than a carpet like thyme or chamomile, but slight undulations make it rather interesting.

If you absolutely must have grass, then adapt the same idea and grow it surrounded with paving or bricks, set just slightly lower than the top of the soil so that you can mow over it very easily and avoid time-consuming edging. Choose one of the new, slower-growing grass seeds on the market, and if your garden is in shade, buy one that's especially bred for shady places.

In a larger front garden where trees create a lot of shade, you might also think about a wild flower meadow mixture. This would be a better bet – and much less work – than a conventional lawn that's never going to look good. Select a mixture that's suitable for shade and plant spring-flowering bulbs suitable for naturalising like crocus, species daffodils, snake's head fritillary, snowdrops and winter aconites. There will be enough light for them to thrive before the trees come into full leaf, and all the attention the area will need is one going-over with a power scythe in mid-summer.

When it comes to choosing materials for your hard landscaping there are several factors to be borne in mind. First, it should be in keeping with the house. If your house is brick that doesn't mean you have to use the same bricks for all the hard landscaping and, indeed, it might look a bit overpowering. But if you put down paving slabs that blend with the colour of the brick and use the bricks as an edging or to replace the occasional slab it will have a unity with the house. If you live in a period house, the real thing may be prohibitively expensive but there's nothing to stop you adapting modern materials to achieve the right sort of effect.

You also have to bear in mind that the hard landscaping in the front garden is as much decorative as functional, and so you should use the most attractive materials you can find. That doesn't necessarily mean the most expensive – some of the imitation York stone substitutes now available are as attractive as the real thing, and of a fraction of the price, and if you live in an older house, second hand bricks from an architectural salvage firm could be perfect for the job.

Gravel is an excellent choice for a low-maintenance front garden (see page 124), especially in a mainly ornamental area which doesn't get walked on very much.

Raised beds are also easy-care because the plants are at a convenient height for tending – and enjoying – and there is no weeding, since what soil you have is covered with plants. They are also an opportunity to grow any plants you like: even if you have alkaline soil in the garden, you can fill the raised beds with special compost for acid-loving plants and grow dwarf rhododendrons, or summer-flowering heathers (*Calluna vulgaris*).

PREPARATIONS FOR A LOW-MAINTENANCE GARDEN

Perhaps the most important point to bear in mind before you start is that creating a low-maintenance garden is labour-intensive and comparatively expensive. But remember, what you're doing is spending in one short, sharp burst all the effort and cash that an ordinary garden would cost over a number of years. Once it's done and the plants have had a chance to grow a bit, it takes very little work – or cash – to keep it looking good for many years ahead.

It is important to plan your garden very carefully, and be as sure as possible that the design is one that you'll be happy with for the foreseeable future. In an ordinary garden, if the lawn isn't the right shape, it's easily and cheaply rectified with a sharp spade and perhaps a bit of grass seed; if the hard landscaping turns out to be the wrong shape, or you find that the steps are in the wrong place, it's very expensive to put it right.

It also means preparing the ground very carefully even if you're going to have an area paved. Weeds like mare's tail, couch grass and Japanese knotweed can certainly push

A vast improvement on the plain custard-coloured concrete slabs that were there before, our low-maintenance garden is attractive both from the street (*below*) and from the front door (*left*).

their way up between paving slabs, and can even penetrate concrete, so it pays dividends to clean the ground as thoroughly as you can (see page 123).

Another important rule of low-maintenance gardening is, don't fight nature. Once the ground is clear, check what sort of soil you have (see page 124). Trying to grow plants that don't like the conditions you're offering is a waste of time and money, and also very frustrating. So if you don't have an acid soil, forget rhododendrons and all the summer-flowering heathers (unless, of course, you're going to build raised beds and can import the lime-free soil they like) and concentrate on the many other equally beautiful plants which like neutral or alkaline soil.

What you are aiming to do is prepare the soil so well, making it weed-free, well-drained and yet moisture-rententive, and so fertile, that once you've put in the plants you won't need to do anything more to it for years, except give it an annual sprinkle of some slow-release fertiliser like bonemeal (look for a coarse-ground grade rather than a fine one; it takes even longer to break down) and a top-up of mulch.

LOW-MAINTENANCE PLANTS

When it comes to choosing the plants for your low-maintenance garden, select those that will be happy in the conditions you offer, that will grow reasonably slowly or will spread to cover the ground, so that it's impossible for weeds to push their way through, and will virtually take care of themselves. That rules out anything that needs staking, tying, supporting, regularly dividing or pruning, protecting from the weather, spraying against diseases or defending from pests.

It also rules out anything that's too rampant. While, initially, something like snow-in-summer (*Cerastium tomentosum*) or dead nettle (*Lamium galeobdolon*) may seem the answer to a maiden's prayer as it spreads across the ground at a rate of knots, it will quickly get out of hand, start throttling other plants and will need frequent hacking back – which is high maintenance.

You will also probably be buying large shrubs rather than small ones, and three or five perennials rather than just one. Again, this is expensive. A cheaper way is to buy small shrubs and wait for them to grow to a reasonable size, or to buy one perennial, plant it, wait for a year or two until it grows, then divide it up into three or five, replant the divisions and wait for them to knit together into a ground-covering clump. But that's not low-maintenance, nor is filling the gaps with colourful annuals – and nor is keeping those wide-open spaces free from weeds.

But even if you do plant densely, there will still be some gaps between plants for a season or two while they get established and start to knit together to form an impenetrable carpet. To many of us, weeding is a chore, the horticultural equivalent of washing-up; so to minimise it, the answer is to mulch. This means spreading a thick layer of something like chipped or shredded bark over the surface of the soil to keep out the light and so discourage any remaining perennial weeds from appearing and prevent annual weeds from germinating.

You could use virtually anything to keep the light out but in the low-maintenance garden, where looks are as important as function, bark chippings (not composted bark which is a good soil conditioner but breaks down too quickly for low-maintenance mulching) is a good bet. You'll need a layer at least 10cm (4in) thick. The one drawback is that it's expensive, although it should last a couple of seasons and then will only need topping up rather than replacing altogether.

A mulching product based on cocoa shells is now available and *Gardening from Which?* found that in their trials it outperformed all other mulches for improving plant growth, conserving moisture and suppressing weeds. It also has the advantage of releasing a sort of gum once it's become wet, which holds the fragments together and stops them blowing about the garden. And it's wonderful if you're a chocoholic, since it smells strongly of chocolate! Again, the one snag is cost – slightly more than bark chippings.

If money is no object, though, you can now buy 'designer mulch' – wood chips dyed in a range of colours from natural to green and honey – which will cost you almost as much per square metre as the best tufted Wilton! But for a very small area in a very small garden, it could be just the special touch that makes all the difference.

A cheaper alternative is to cover the area to be planted with newspapers, black polythene or a new woven planting membrane, then plant through holes cut in it, and when the whole area is planted, hide the underlayer with a thin layer of bark, cocoa shells, wood chips or gravel. As for watering, newspaper will absorb water and release it into the soil, and the new planting membrane allows water to penetrate, but black polythene does create problems since only a little water will penetrate through the slits you've cut and the rest will trickle off and go to waste. But these problems can be overcome if you install a porous rubber hose under the polythene (see easy watering below).

Watering is another garden chore. The most labour intensive method is simply to stand there holding the hose, and it's also the least effective, because few people have the patience to stand there for long enough to give the plants the amount of water they need! Hose-end sprinklers certainly remove the tedium but unless you have a really small garden you still have to move them several times to make sure all the plants get watered, and, as we become ever more conscious that water is a precious resource, it is a very wasteful method.

The best solution is to install an automatic watering system. One type is based on seep hoses, which are specially manufactured porous rubber hoses that allow the water to seep out very slowly along their entire length. Another is a micro-irrigation system, using flexible plastic tubing of different thicknesses with an adjustable nozzle at the end, which are linked together on or just below the surface of the soil to deliver water at an easily controlled rate to individual trees and shrubs and to clumps of herbaceous plants. That way the water goes to where it's most needed. You can also fit sensors to the system which will detect when the soil is dry and open the valves to allow the water to start dripping again.

Micro-irrigation systems are flexible enough to service containers, too, so that the whole garden can be watered with one single turn of a tap. The cost for an average sized garden starts at around £40. With both systems, you can even fit an automatic timer to turn on the water for you. The timers cost about £70.

All you have to do, having spent the money, is hope that we don't have another hosepipe ban this summer – although spending money on a watering system is probably a very good way to ensure a really wet summer, and besides, the manufacturers of these systems are talking to the water authorities about getting them made exempt from hosepipe bans, since they are so economical in their use of water.

LOW-MAINTENANCE TREES

To qualify for inclusion in a low-maintenance front garden, a tree must be small, slow-growing; not need pruning or training or protecting from the weather; be resistant to pests and diseases; and, ideally, should not make any mess by shedding leaves, petals or berries. That last stipulation would rule out everything but evergreens and, apart from conifers, there are few good, small evergreen trees. Since it would also rule out on all three counts the flowering cherries, the ornamental crabs and the rowans, which are among the best trees for small gardens, it's probably best ignored!

The heights and spreads given for these trees, incidentally, are for those growing in ideal conditions of rich deep moist, loamy soil and plenty of space. In thin, poor soils, or where their root run is restricted, they won't achieve that size.

The Paperbark maple (*Acer griseum*)
A near-perfect tree for a small garden, because it has so many good qualities – attractive orange-buff foliage in spring, glorious autumn colour and, in winter, on wood that's at least three years old, the orange-brown bark peels away to reveal the new cinnamon-coloured bark beneath. Its ascending branches and rather open habit allow light to reach plants growing underneath it. It's also very slow-growing.
Approx. height and spread after five years: 2 × 1.2 m (6 × 4 ft). After 20 years: 6 × 3 m (20 × 10 ft).

Acer pseudoplatanus ('Brilliantissimum')

A very slow-growing small tree with stunning spring foliage opening deep shrimp-pink, becoming paler flesh pink, then creamy-yellow and pale green before assuming its summer mid-green. Its only fault is that it's rather dull the rest of the year.

Approx. height and spread after five years: 2.5 × 1.5m (8 × 5ft). After 20 years: 4.5 × 3.5m (14ft 6in × 12ft).

Weeping cotoneaster *(Cotoneaster × hybridus pendulus)*

An excellent choice for a low-maintenance garden, this truly mini semi-evergreen tree has masses of small white flowers in spring followed by bunches of small red fruits in autumn and winter. Ideal for a tiny garden or a container.

Approx. height and spread after five years: 2.5 × 1.2m (8 × 4ft). After 20 years: 3 × 4m (10 × 13ft).

Flowering thorn *(Crataegus laevigata* 'Paul's Double Scarlet' aka 'Coccinea Plena')

A small, round-headed tree with dark pinky-red double flowers in late spring and early summer and a few small red berries in the autumn. Less widely available, though very attractive, is the double pink flowered variety *C.l.* 'Rosea Flore Pleno'.

Approx. height and spread after five years: 4 × 1.2m (13 × 4ft). After 20 years: 6 × 6m (20 × 20ft).

Golden honey locust *(Gleditsia triacanthos* 'Sunburst')

Perhaps the best golden foliage tree there is, with feathery foliage that is bright gold when it first appears. It is prone to wind damage so does best in a sheltered spot. Less well known, but also attractive, is *G.t.* 'Elegantissima', which has fresh green fern-like foliage and only reaches about half the height and spread of 'Sunburst'. It's harder to find, though.

Approx. height and spread of 'Sunburst' after five years: 3 × 1.5m (10 × 5ft). After 20 years: 7 × 5m (23 × 16ft).

MAGNOLIA

These form large shrubs or small trees and are grown for their stunning flowers which usually appear before the leaves in spring. The best varieties for larger front gardens include *M.* × *loebneri* 'Leonard Messel' which has deep mauve-pink buds opening to a paler pink and *M.* × *soulangiana* 'Alba Superba' which has white cup-shaped flowers.

Approx. height and spread after five years: 2 × 2m (6 × 6ft). After 20 years: 7 × 8m (23 × 26ft).

For smaller gardens the Star Magnolia (*M. stellata*), which is smothered in narrow-petalled white flowers in spring, is a good choice.

Approx. height and spread after five years: 80cm × 1m (2ft 6in × 3ft). After 20 years: 2.5 × 3.5m (8 × 12ft).

This front garden needs very little maintenance because the plants are so close together that weeds don't get the chance to become established.

ORNAMENTAL CRAB APPLES (*MALUS*)

There are many excellent varieties of ornamental crab suitable for small front gardens with masses of flowers in spring, in some cases attractively coloured foliages, and bright coloured fruits in autumn.

Malus sargentii
One of the smaller and slower-growing crabs, it has masses of scented white flowers (tinted yellow in bud) with golden stamens. In autumn it has bright red currant-like fruits and its leaves turn yellow.
Approx. height and spread after five years: 1.5m × 70cm (5 × 2ft). After 20 years: 5 × 2m (16 × 6ft).

Malus 'Golden Hornet'
Its white flowers are followed by bright yellow fruits in autumn. For some reason, birds prefer red and orange fruits to yellow, so these usually get left alone until well into the winter.
Approx. height and spread after five years: 4 × 1.5m (13 × 5ft). After 20 years: 8 × 6m (26 × 20ft).

Malus 'Profusion'

As well as its coppery-crimson young foliage which slowly turns green through the summer, it also has purply-red flowers which fade to pink and oxblood red fruits.
Approx. height and spread after five years: 4 × 1.5 m (13 × 5 ft). After 20 years: 8 × 6 m (26 × 20 ft).

Malus 'Red Jade'

A small weeping crab with bright green leaves which turn yellow in autumn, then blush-white flowers followed by small bright red fruits.
Approx. height and spread after five years: 2 × 1.5 m (6 × 5 ft). After 20 years: 3 × 5 m (10 × 16 ft).

FLOWERING CHERRIES, PLUMS AND ALMONDS (PRUNUS)

This species offers an even wider choice than the Ornamental crabs, though avoid the spectacular double flowered varieties like the Dame-Barbara-Cartland pink *Prunus* 'Kanzan', which you often see in streets and parks or, too often, completely filling small front gardens. They flower for a couple of weeks, shed their petals everywhere and then offer very little of interest for the rest of the year.

Some breeders are now offering Japanese flowering cherries grafted on to dwarfing rootstocks, which means the final height and spread of the tree is reduced. Before you buy, it's worth checking on to which sort of rootstock your tree is grafted.

'Yoshino cherry' (Prunus × yedoensis)

This makes a graceful small tree with arching branches and masses of almond-scented blush-white flowers in late March-early April. It also has good autumn colour.
Approx. height and spread after five years: 3 × 2 m (10 × 6 ft). After 20 years: 7 × 5 m (23 × 16 ft).

Tibetan cherry (Prunus serrula)

Although this has masses of small white flowers in May, its main claim to fame is its superb mahogany coloured bark which peels away to reveal a patina as smooth as superb antique furniture. It takes between five and ten years for this to develop.
Approx. height and spread after five years: 4 × 2 m (13 × 6 ft). After 20 years: 7 × 4 m (23 × 13 ft).

The autumn cherry (Prunus subhirtella 'Autumnalis')

You often see this tree in front gardens. It produces semi-double white flowers on bare stems from November intermittently right through the winter to April, depending on the weather. It has good golden autumn colour too. There is also an attractive variety with pink flowers *P.s.* 'Autumnalis Rosea'.
Approx. height and spread after five years: 1.5 × 2 m (5 × 6 ft). After 20 years: 7 × 7 m (24 × 24 ft).

Lombardy cherry (*Prunus serrulata* 'Amanogawa')
This tall, narrow tree offers pale candy-pink flowers in spring and its foliage turns gold and flame in autumn. A popular choice for small front gardens because it is so narrow.
Approx. height and spread after five years: 3 × 1m (10 × 3ft). After 20 years: 6 × 2.2m (20 × 7ft).

Prunus × *yedoensis* '**Shidare Yoshino**'
This has masses of pale pink flowers, fading to white, on branches that weep to the ground in early spring. *P.* × *y.* 'Ivensii' has fragrant snow-white flowers and a similar habit.
Approx. height and spread after five years: 3 × 3m (10 × 10ft). After 20 years: 5 × 6m (16 × 20ft).

Weeping willow-leafed pear (*Pyrus salicifolia* 'Pendula')
It does have small white flowers in April but it is grown primarily for the dense mound of silvery foliage it eventually forms.
Approx. height and spread after five years: 2.5 × 2m (8 × 6ft). After 20 years: 4 × 3m (13 × 10ft).

Kilmarnock willow (*Salix caprea* 'Pendula')
Another very small weeping tree, not reaching more than 2–3m (6–10ft) in height. At its most attractive in winter and spring when brown buds along the length of each weeping stem, like a beaded hair-do, open and reveal silver-white, then golden catkins. However, the foliage that follows isn't very exciting.
Approx. height and spread after five years: 2 × 1.5m (6 × 5ft). After 20 years: 3 × 3m (10 × 10ft).

ROWANS

Sorbus
Another family with many members which really earn their keep in small gardens since they have flowers, pretty foliage, good autumn colour and berries.

Kashmir mountain ash (*Sorbus cashmiriana*)
A stunning little tree with very pale pink flowers in spring and fern-like foliage which turns red in autumn, and clusters of pearl-white berries in winter. Its open habit means it only casts dappled shade, so many other plants will grow happily beneath it.
Approx. height and spread after five years: 2 × 2m (6 × 6ft). After 20 years: 4 × 4m (13 × 13ft).

Sorbus vilmorinii
This makes a slightly larger tree than 'Cashmiriana', but has similar white flowers in spring and delicate ferny foliage which turns purply-red in autumn. Its berries, which hang in clusters, start out a rosy red, then fade slowly from pink to white.
Approx. height and spread after five years: 2.5 × 1.5m (8 × 5ft). After 20 years: 6 × 3m (20 × 10ft).

CONIFERS

Conifers make excellent specimen trees for low-maintenance gardens because they are evergreen and they really do look after themselves. The one proviso, and it is a very important one, is that you really do make sure that you buy a *dwarf* conifer. You don't have to drive very far in any town to see conifers in front gardens which *weren't* dwarf varieties and so are now filling the whole garden, blocking out all the light. Dwarf conifers are very, very slow growing and so they are usually sold as young, very small plants. As you want your garden to have an impact right away and to start looking after itself, it's worth paying the extra and buying a specimen that's five or even 10 years old. All those listed shouldn't reach more than 2m (6ft 6in) in 10 years.

Chamaecyparis lawsoniana 'Ellwood's Gold'
This forms a pyramid of gold tinged foliage about 1.2m (4ft) tall.

Chamaecyparis lawsoniana 'Little Spire'
This one is a narrow upright pillar of bright green foliage which grows to about 2m (6ft 6in).

Chamaecyparis pisifera 'Boulevard'
Grow this one for its intense silvery blue foliage. It forms a broad-based pyramid up to 1.2m (4ft) tall.

Juniperus chinensis 'Pyramidalis'
Another excellent silver-blue conifer forming a much narrower pyramid this time, up to 2m (6ft 6in) tall.

Juniperus scopulorum 'Skyrocket'
A very tall upright conifer with blue-grey foliage reaching just over 2m (7ft) but so narrow that it doesn't take up too much space even in a very small garden.

Irish Yew (*Taxus baccata* 'Standishii')
A very slow-growing narrow column of gold foliage, it won't ever reach more than 1.5m (5ft).

Taxus baccata 'Fastigiata Robusta'
This is a very dark green version of the one above reaching the same height or even a little more (1.6m (5ft)).

The cool combination of white walls and blue paintwork provide an ideal background for a riot of spring colour.

Thuja occidentalis 'Marrison Sulphur'
This has very attractive lacy creamy yellow foliage and eventually forms a pyramid up to 2 m (6 ft 6 in) tall.

Thuja occidentalis 'Rheingold'
One of the best golden conifers, forming a very broad-based pyramid with bright gold leaves in summer and rich coppery gold in winter. It reaches 1.2 m (4 ft) eventually.

LOW-MAINTENANCE CLIMBERS

The perfect low-maintenance climber is self-supporting (or at least, once pointed in the right direction, can manage without further help from you), isn't too vigorous and won't clog up your gutters. That rules out things like Russian Vine, the more rampant clematis like *C. montana* and roses like *R. filipes* 'Kiftsgate' and 'Albertine'. However that still leaves you plenty of other excellent climbers to choose from.

Clematis
For low-maintenance gardening, the best varieties are the small flowered types which grow happily through other shrubs so need no support and which need little or no pruning. Varieties of *C. alpina*, for instance, which have nodding blue, pink or white flowers in spring, are marvellous growing through evergreen shrubs. Look for the large blue and white flowered *C.a.* 'Frances Rivis', the white *C.a.* 'White Columbine' and the pink *C.a.* 'Willy'. The slightly later flowering *C. macropetala* is also an excellent choice; look for the double blue-flowered *C.m.* 'Maidwell Hall' and the pink *C.m.* 'Markhamii' (sometimes sold as 'Markham's Pink'). Both alpinas and macropetalas reach about 2.5 m (8 ft) and need no pruning unless they outgrow their allotted space.

The late-flowering *C. viticella*, with small flowers in wine-red (*C.v.* 'Mme Julia Correvon'), purple (*C.v.* 'Purpurea Plena Elegans') or white (*C.v.* 'Alba Luxurians'); *C. texensis*, with flowers of deep pink (*C.t.* 'Duchess of Albany') or the ruby-red (*C.* × 'Gravetye Beauty') are also ideal for growing through other shrubs. The former can be left to ramble or cut back hard in spring to 30 cm (1 ft) from the ground – a couple of snips with the secateurs. The latter should be cut hard back in spring.

Climbing hydrangea (*Hydrangea petiolaris*)
A marvellous self-clinging climber for all soil types, it does as well in shade as in sun. It would be worth growing just for the masses of bright, fresh green leaves it produces each spring but it also has large flat heads of white flowers in early summer which turn brown in autumn and remain, attractively, on the bare stems in winter.
Approx. height and spread after 10 years: 3 × 4m + (10 × 13ft +).

Ivy *(Hedera)*

This is the best evergreen climber. It is self-clinging, happy in deep shade and tolerates all kinds of soil. One of the variegated kinds, like the small-leafed bright gold green *H. helix* 'Goldheart' or the much larger leafed *H. colchica* 'Paddy's Pride', really would brighten up a dark wall or fence. If you want a plain green, as a background for variegated shrubs, perhaps, then the glossy *H.h.* 'Hibernica' is ideal. Ivy is also excellent low-maintenance ground cover among shrubs and trees. Small-leafed varieties like the curly-leafed 'Ivalace', 'Conglomerata' and the variegated 'Heise' can be used in a formal setting, as a grass-substitute, although it will need trimming once a year to keep it neat.
Approx. height and spread after five years: 4m (13ft). After 10 years: 5m (16ft).

Honeysuckle *(Lonicera)*

A twining plant like this is best grown up an arch or through trellis or an old tree where it can use the twigs and branches to support itself. It will need tying in, just to get it started. Try either the early or late Dutch honeysuckle *L. periclymenum* 'Belgica' and 'Serotina' respectively, which have large sweetly-scented flowers. Gold-netted Japanese honeysuckle *L. japonica* 'Aureo-reticulata', which has attractive semi-evergreen foliage as well as sweetly-scented small yellow flowers in summer, does well in shade. It can be neglected for four or five years, then a quick going-over with the shears, removing a lot of the forward-growing shoots after flowering, will keep it going with renewed vigour.
Approx. height and spread: 3.5–8m (12–26ft).

Roses

The ideal low-maintenance climber is a repeat-flowerer of only moderate vigour, with stiff stems that can be tied against a fence or wall initially and then left pretty well alone. They include the pretty pink 'Aloha', the red 'Dublin Bay', 'White Cockade' and the yellow 'Golden Showers'. None of them will grow to more than about 2.5m (8ft) so that any work – dead heading, maybe, or cutting out dead wood – can be done standing on the ground or from a pair of low steps. As an alternative, try one of the new miniature climbers like the yellow 'Laura Ford' or the orange 'Warm Welcome' which have smaller leaves and flowers than an ordinary climber and won't grow to more than 2m (6ft).

Virginia creeper *(Parthenocissus)*

Although all types of this self-clinging climber have wonderful autumn colour *P. henryana* gives the best value for several reasons. First, it has the most beautiful dark velvety green leaves deeply veined with silver and pink in spring and summer; and second, it's not as vigorous as some of the other Virginia creepers and so is unlikely to cause problems with blocked gutters or roof tiles. It's happiest in part-shade or shade.
Approx. height and spread after 10 years: 6 × 6m (20 × 20ft).

LOW-MAINTENANCE SHRUBS

Again, to earn a place in this section a shrub must be able to give a good show for as long as possible and to take care of itself. Its ability to form an impenetrable weed-proof layer, is also a huge plus. Some shrubs, like broom, don't have a long life so are best avoided in permanent low-maintenance planting. But they can be useful to fill in between bigger permanent shrubs for a few years until the latter take up their allotted space.

Spotted laurel (*Aucuba japonica*)

One of the most accommodating of all evergreen shrubs, it will grow happily in practically any type of soil and will also tolerate deep shade. Look for *A.j.* 'Crotonifolia', which has large leaves speckled with gold, and 'Variegata' whose smaller leaves are splashed with gold and yellow over about half their area. It grows quite large, but you can cut it back, so it's a good choice for the back of a border or a very shady corner.

Approx. height and spread after 10 years: 1.8 × 1.8m (5.5 × 5.5ft).

Barberry (*Berberis*)

They have different coloured foliage – gold, red, red and pink, as well as green, flowers in spring, then berries and, in many cases, good foliage colour in autumn. The best ground-covering ones are *B. thunbergii* 'Green Carpet' and *B.t.* 'Dart's Red Lady', which, with deep purple leaves that turn a vivid fiery red in autumn, is hard to beat.

Approx. height and spread after 10 years: 1.8 × 1.5m (5.5 × 5ft).

Camellia

If you have an acid soil, these are first class shrubs for a front garden, and will delight both you and the neighbourhood during February to April. They have spectacular single, semi-double or double flowers in a whole range of colours from white, through many shades of pink, to blood-red (and even a few multi-colours like the pink and white striped *C. japonica* 'Lady Vansittart'). Once the flowers have fallen their elegant glossy green leaves are attractive in their own right. They need shelter from icy north and east winds and the early morning sun can frost their buds, so don't plant them in an east facing position. They are happiest in dappled shade.

Good varieties include: White flowers *Camellia japonica* 'Alba Plena'. Pink flowers the soft pink semi-double *C.j.* 'Lady Clare'; the clear rich pink *C.j.* 'Leonard Messel'; and perhaps the most widely grown and popular of all *C.* × *williamsii* 'Donation', with large semi-double clear pink flowers from February onwards. Red flowers *C.j.* 'Adolphe Audusson' whose semi-double blood-red flowers have conspicuous gold stamens.

Approx. height and spread after 10 years: 1.5 × 1.5m (5 × 5ft). For Japonica types: *Williamsii* grow larger up to 3 × 1.5m (10 × 5ft).

Californian lilac *(Ceanothus)*

When smothered with bright blue thimbles of flowers in early summer, it is a startling sight. There are both evergreen and deciduous kinds, but for the low-maintenance garden the evergreens are the best bet, though they're not totally hardy in colder areas or very severe winters. Among the hardiest and/or smallest-growing evergreen varieties are *C. impressus* with distinctive small glossy green leaves and masses of small deep blue flowers in late spring, and Creeping blue blossom (*C. thyrsiflorus* 'Repens') which very quickly forms a mound of dense, weed-suppressing evergreen foliage and is covered in mid-blue blossom in May.

Approx. height and spread after 10 years: *C. impressus* 1.5 × 3m (5 × 10ft). *C. thyrsiflorus* 'Repens' 1 × 2.5m (3 × 8ft).

Mexican orange blossom *(Choisya ternata)*

A valuable low-maintenance shrub with its glossy aromatic evergreen leaves and profusion of small white scented flowers in summer and often again in autumn. It will grow in shade as well as full sun, though it flowers more freely in the latter position. It forms a large rounded bush but can be pruned to keep it within the allotted space. There is also a new golden variety *C.t.* 'Sundance', just over half the size of its parent and more tender. It doesn't like deep shade and some people also find that the flowers aren't as fragrant. An even newer variety, *C.t.* 'Aztec Pearl', has much more slender aromatic green leaves, white flowers, pink in bud, and reaches much the same size as 'Sundance'.

Approx. height and spread after 10 years: 2 × 1.8m (6 × 5.5ft).

Smoke bush *(Cotinus coggygria)*

This good shrub for a large garden gets its common name from the clouds of tiny flowers that cover it all summer, turning a smoky grey in the autumn. The purple leafed varieties, like *C.c.* 'Royal Purple' or 'Notcutt's Variety', are the most stunning with wine-red foliage in spring and summer and superb autumn colour too.

Approx. height and spread after 10 years: 3 × 3m (10 × 10ft).

Cotoneaster

There are deciduous and evergreen varieties to suit most situations. Many of the evergreens are good for low-maintenance gardens, especially the small-leafed, ground-cover types which can cope with full sun and shade. Look for *C. dammeri* ('Coral Beauty' is particularly good), with white flowers in summer followed by red berries. The slow-growing *C. microphyllus*, good for covering a bank or for growing over a wall, has masses of tiny grey-green leaves, white flowers in early summer and dark red fruits in autumn, and forms a low mound rather than growing completely flat like *C.dammeri*.

Approx. height and spread after 10 years: 30–60cm × 2m (1–2 × 6ft).

Escallonia

A valuable late-summer-flowering evergreen shrub, and useful hedging plant. Good varieties include *E.* 'Donard Seedling' with pale pink flowers, 'Donard Star' with rose-pink flowers, the tall 'Iveyi' with glossy, dark green leaves and large pure white flowers and 'Peach Blossom' with soft peachy-pink flowers. It's particularly good in seaside areas.

Approx. height and spread after 10 years: 2 × 1.8 m (6 × 5 ft).

Spindle *(Euonymus fortunei)*

A versatile evergreen shrub for sun or shade that will either climb up a wall if pointed in the right direction or make excellent ground cover. There are several good variegated forms. Among the green-and-golds, look for *E.f.* 'Emerald 'n' Gold' and 'Gold Tip', and for the quieter cream-and-greens, the best is *E.f.* 'Emerald Gaiety'. For climbing try *E.f.* 'Variegatus' whose leaves are flushed pink in very cold weather.

Approx. height and spread after 10 years: 60 cm × 2 m (2 × 6 ft). Climbing: after 10 years: up to 4 × 4 m (13 × 13 ft).

False caster oil plant *(Fatsia japonica)*

It is often thought of as a houseplant, but in fact it is very hardy and thrives in deep to medium shade. It's an architectural shrub, used for the bold, dramatic shape of its large, handsome, glossy evergreen leaves. In spring it produces spikes of creamy-white flowers rather like golf balls which eventually turn into clusters of black berries.

Approx. height and spread after 10 years: 2 × 2 m (6 × 6 ft).

Shrubby veronicas *(Hebe)*

Some of the smaller evergreen hebes are first class ground-covering shubs with very attractive foliage as well as flowers in early summer – the blue-grey *H. pinguifolia* 'Pagei', for example, and the mound-forming *H. albicans*, with densely packed, small elliptical grey-green leaves. Neither will reach more than 50 cm × 1 m (1 ft 6 in × 3 ft) in 10 years. Of the larger hebes *H.* 'Midsummer Beauty', *H.* × *franciscana* 'Blue Gem' and *H.* 'Autumn Glory', which all have mauve or lavender-blue flowers at various times throughout the summer, and the pink-flowered compact, *H.* 'Great Orme', are all good. There are lovely variegated varieties too, like *H.* × *andersonii* or *H.* × *franciscana* 'Variegata', but they are even less hardy than their plainer relatives.

Approx. height and spread after 10 years: 1.5 × 1.5 m (5 × 5 ft).

Hypericum calycinum (rose of Sharon)

This is often recommended for quick ground cover but unless you have lots of ground to cover it's best avoided, since it simply doesn't know where to stop! A better bet for a small garden is the semi-evergreen *H. patulum* 'Hidcote'.

Approx. height and spread after 10 years (of *H.p.* 'Hidcote'): 1.2 × 1.2 m (4 × 4 ft).

Shrubby potentilla (*P. fruticosa*)

These make small to medium-sized rounded bushes which carry their small pretty open-faced flowers for months on end. They flower even better if they are given a quick trim with the shears in the autumn every year of two. Among the best are: the yellow-flowered 'Katherine Dykes' or 'Elizabeth'; the pure white-flowered 'Abbotswood', with soft grey foliage; the smallest-growing, cream-flowered 'Tilford Cream'; and some of the newer ones like the orange-red 'Red Ace' and the pale pink 'Princess', whose flowers fade in prolonged hot dry weather to near-white.

Approx. height and spread after 10 years: 1 × 1m (3 × 3ft).

Pieris

If you have an acid soil, these are perhaps the ideal evergreen shrubs for a very small garden because they really do earn their keep. In spring, tassels of small white flowers, rather like lily-of-the-valley, open at the same time as the new foliage is coming through. The new, slender, spear-shaped leaves start out a vivid shade of scarlet, slowly fade through pink, cream and pale green before acquiring their glossy summer mid-green. The clusters of small red buds for next season's flowers which form in the autumn add brightness during the winter months.

Look out for *P. formosa* 'Wakehurst' which has shorter, broader leaves than most but superb spring colour, *P. forrestii* 'Forest Flame', one of the hardiest varieties with particularly bright new foliage, and *P. japonica* 'Variegata' whose leaves are creamy-white, flushed with pink when they first open. It's slower growing than most and forms a smaller shrub – about ⅔rds the average height and spread.

Approx. height and spread after 10 years: 1.5 × 2m (5 × 6ft).

Pyracantha (*Firethorn*)

This is an ideal shrub for training against a shady wall, with its glossy evergreen leaves, white flowers in early summer and clusters of yellow, orange or red berries in autumn. Good varieties to look out for include: *P.* 'Mojave', with orange-red berries; *P.* 'Orange Glow', with very dark foliage and lots of orange berries and *P.* 'Soleil d'Or', with mid-green leaves and deep yellow berries.

Height and spread after 10 years: 3.5 × 2m (12 × 6ft).

Rhododendron

For a front garden with an acid soil, or for containers, there are some excellent dwarf rhododendrons around. Look out for 'Blue Tit' with violet-blue flowers, 'Pink Drift' with lavender-pink flowers and aromatic olive-green leaves, 'Scarlet Wonder' with trumpet-shaped, frilly red flowers or 'Moonstone' with rosy-crimson buds opening to a creamy pale primrose yellow. *R. yakushimanum* is a stunner; not only does it have masses

The star of this small front garden is a Japanese maple, grown as a standard.
The sun shining through its new red foliage in the spring makes
it positively glow.

of rose pink buds opening to apple blossom pink flowers which slowly fade to white but its foliage is striking too, with long narrow leathery leaves that are silvery at first, turning a really dark glossy green on top with woolly brown undersides. Its many hybrids like 'Doc', 'Grumpy', 'Silver Sixpence' and 'Surrey Heath' have superb flowers in a range of striking colours but none has the same beautiful foliage as the parent. They all do best in dappled shade.

Approx. height and spread after 10 years: 80 cm × 1 m (2 × 3 ft).

Roses

The most widely grown roses – the **hybrid teas** – are not low-maintenance because of all the pruning and spraying involved. If you want roses, go for shrub roses which don't need regular pruning, like 'Marjorie Fair', 'Ballerina' or the pretty creamy white 'Anna Zinkeisen'; or flat ground cover roses like 'Snow Carpet', 'Nozomi' and 'Suma', 'Grouse' and 'Pheasant' or from the new 'County' series, 'Surrey', 'Sussex' and 'Norfolk' which form quite large dense mounds of ground-covering foliage. Although you don't need to remove dead flowers for the sake of the plants, they do look neater if you do. Anyway, dead-heading counts more as 'pottering' than real work!

Approx. height and spread after five years: 80 cm–1.2 m × 80 cm–1.2 m (2.5–4 × 2.5–4 ft).

The new patio or dwarf roses (different breeders sell them under different names) are also very good for low-maintenance gardens since they don't need pruning and many are good bushy plants which makes them useful ground cover. Again there are many good ones to choose from and more are being introduced all the time. Among the best patio roses are the pale rose-pink 'Gentle Touch', the apricot-pink 'Peek a Boo' and the old favourite, 'The Fairy' with masses of clear pink rosettes from July to Christmas given a mild autumn. One of the newest is a dwarf shrub rose (or 'shrublet' Ugh!) 'Little Bo Peep' which makes a very bushy spreading ground-cover plant covered in pale pink flowers all summer.

Approx. height and spread after five years: 50–60 × 40–60 cm (18 in–2 ft × 15 in–2 ft).

Christmas box (*Sarcococca humilis*)

A good dwarf evergreen ground-covering shrub that has narrow pointed glossy green leaves and sweetly scented small white flowers as early as February – a bonus in the front garden. It needs a rich soil but will tolerate some alkalinity and will grow in deep shade though it does better with a little more light.

Height and spread after 10 years: 50 × 50 cm (19 × 19 in).

Skimmia

This is another invaluable small evergreen shrub, for sun or shade, provided it gets the right soil conditions – it won't tolerate any lime and dislikes extremes of waterlogging and drought. It has shiny aromatic leaves, scented white flowers in late spring, and clusters of shiny red or white berries in autumn. To be sure of berries you need to plant at least one male with any number of females. Good varieties include *S. japonica* 'Nymans' or × 'Foremanii' (both female) and *S.j.* 'Rubella', a male form which has fat short pokers of deep red buds which open to blush-white sweetly scented flowers. *S. reevesiana* is self-fertile.

Height and spread after 10 years: 60 × 60 cm (2 × 2 ft).

Viburnum

The best ground-cover member of the family is *V. davidii*, an attractive low spreading evergreen shrub with large leathery dark green leaves and glossy white flowers in June followed by striking turquoise fruits – provided there is a male plant around to pollinate the female. It's not easy to be sure you've got bushes of both sexes but if you have enough room plant at least three and increase the odds!

Approx. height and spread after 10 years: 1.2 × 1.2 m (4 × 4 m).

Lesser periwinkle (*Vinca minor*)
This is an excellent evergreen ground-covering shrub for those difficult dry shady places – under trees and taller shrubs for example. It flowers from April to June and among the best varieties are the blue-flowered 'Bowles Variety', the variegated 'Elegantissima' and the lovely pure white 'Gertrude Jekyll'. If you've got a large area to cover you could go for the greater periwinkle (*V. major*), which is most attractive in its variegated form.
Approx. height and spread after 10 years: 15 × 60 cm (6 in × 2 ft).

LOW-MAINTENANCE PERENNIALS: GROUND-COVER

Again, the plants you choose must be able to take care of themselves and to carpet the ground so that no weed can even *think* about getting established. In low-maintenance gardening, the aim is to cover the ground as quickly as possible. Obviously you could plant all your perennials so that they are almost touching, and within a couple of months, you'll have achieved the desired effect. The downside is that, next year or the year after they would be growing into each other, fighting for survival and dying off. So it's a question of striking a happy medium and planting them slightly closer together than is usually recommended and mulching the bare soil in between.

For a list of excellent low-maintenance ground-cover plants see page 150.

ANNUALS AND BIENNIALS

The only annuals and biennials that qualify for inclusion here are either the half-hardies bought as plants from the garden centre (or by mail order) ready to go straight into the border, or those that self-seed very effectively, so that once you've sown the seed, you never have to bother again. Do remember that seed from F 1 hybrids will not breed true.

Alyssum maritimum
This easy-to-grow annual forms neat mounds of foliage covered in tiny white flowers all summer long. It's an excellent plant to grow between slabs or bricks on a patio or path and re-seeds itself so readily that once you've sown a few, you'll never be without it.

Pot marigolds (*Calendula officinalis*)
These old-fashioned pot marigolds will seed themselves quite happily so simply buy a packet of seeds, sow them directly and very thinly into the soil where you want them to flower, and forget about them.

Californian poppy (*Eschscholzia californica*)
This striking annual has attractive feathery foliage and masses of bright orange flowers throughout the summer. You may find them now in shades of cream and pink but they are likely to revert to orange when self-sown.

Busy Lizzie (*Impatiens*)
Not hardy and so not one to self-seed, but a few plants bought at the end of May, when all danger of frost is past, and planted out in a group, can add an invaluable splash of colour to a largely evergreen low-maintenance border.

Poached Egg Flower (*Limnanthes douglasii*)
This low-growing annual has attractive foliage and yellow saucer-shaped flowers edged with white. It also looks good grown between paving slabs and seeds itself very readily.

Nasturtium (*Tropaeolum majus*)
The ideal low-maintenance plant for very poor dry soils. (In better soils, it produces much more leaf than flower but the leaves are worth having for their ground-covering abilities.) Simply push the large seeds into the soil in spring. It too will seed itself easily.

BULBS

Bulbs are probably the easiest way to bring spring colour to a largely evergreen low-maintenance front garden, *provided* you stick to the types that need little or no attention. That immediately rules out the larger tulips which should be lifted after flowering, dried, stored and re-planted the following autumn. Species tulips, on the other hand, which are just as beautiful if not more so, can be left quite happily in the soil year after year.

Planting bulbs with ground cover is ideal because the dying foliage of the bulbs – never a pretty sight – is hidden or at least disguised to some extent by the ground-cover plants through which they've been growing.

They are also invaluable if you have a shady area under trees (either your own or street trees that cast shade over your front garden) for naturalising in long grass. There is enough light for them to give a good display in the spring before the trees come into leaf.

For a list of suitable crocuses, daffodils and tulips see The Cottage Garden, page 61.

CHAPTER SIX

THE NEW ESTATE GARDEN

*M*any hundreds of thousands of people live in new estates built all over the country during the last ten years. In many cases, the developers have gone to some trouble to give the houses themselves some individuality but all too often the front gardens have a relentless sameness about them – a lawn running straight down to the pavement, a solitary tree, and that's it! To be fair, in many cases, the houses have been sold with restrictive covenants preventing their owners from putting up boundaries and for some people, the feeling that the space isn't really theirs to do with as they like is enough to stop them doing anything at all. Sometimes the covenants are only for a set period, say three or five years, and by the time that's up, inertia has often set in. The owners have got used to the front garden as it is and once they've got the house and back garden as they want it, the motivation to tackle the front has gone.

That wasn't the case with Annette and Glen Wright. They both enjoy gardening, and in the seven years they've been in their semi, they've created a very interesting garden out the back. They had made a number of attempts to do something with the front garden but without success. A clematis Glen planted against the house died and the few daffodils by the front door had been planted with the aid of a chisel!

They suspected the rock-hard soil in the front garden was caused by contractors' vehicles running back and forth across it while the estate was being built, compacting it. A layer of top soil had been spread over the top, just deep enough to support some grass. Since the house faced south, a few long, hot, dry summers had completed the job!

When we started work on the garden, the wettest spring for a long time had softened the top few inches of soil, but it was still virtually impossible to dig down even to one spade's depth, so we brought in a mini-digger, the sort that can be hired from most hire shops. The reason for their problems then became clear – a deep layer of builders' sand plus a scattering of rubble, just below the top soil which had compacted into a solid layer! Annette and Glen were still very keen to try and do something with the front garden. Since there was no boundary between their front garden and their neighbours', Steve and Lorraine Everitt, a communal garden seemed a good idea.

The first thing that designer Roderick Griffin does when he is asked to design a front garden is to ask to see the back garden. That gives him a good indication of how keen on gardening his clients are, how much time they will devote to the front garden, how interested they are in plants and the sorts of things – colours, textures and so forth – that they like. It also tells him which plants will grow in the area – not just what the soil type is, but how protected the area is from frost. In the Wrights' back garden, for example, rhododendrons and pieris were thriving which meant the soil was acid, as were slightly tender shrubs like *Convolvulus cneorum* and × *Halimiocistus*, a very pretty evergreen shrub with pure white flowers in early summer. Since the back garden was north-facing, it seemed likely that even more tender plants would survive in the sunnier, south-facing front.

On a purely practical level, Annette and Glen wanted to do something about the drive since it was so close to the lawn that when drivers and passengers stepped out of the car, they were forced to step onto the grass, which got really muddy in winter. They also wanted to get rid of the lawn altogether. It was patchy, full of weeds and certainly didn't repay the effort of regular mowing. They weren't particularly keen on the maple that had been planted by the developers, and when Rod told them it would eventually grow much too large, they were happy to see it go and be replaced with a smaller tree – something with a much longer season of interest, and a more open habit, so that they could grow a wider range of plants beneath it. The Kashmir rowan (*Sorbus cashmiriana*), which we eventually chose, or the paperbark maple (*Acer griseum*) would be ideal.

Annette and Glen liked the idea of a gravel garden, with colourful plants that looked good all year round, though they were keen to spend some time looking after it. The Everitts were also happy to get rid of the lawn, but wanted a garden that looked after itself. Steve liked the idea of ground cover, but wanted flower colour as well as evergreen foliage.

The challenge that faced Rod Griffin was designing one garden that worked as a whole, but at the same time took account of the different needs of the two sets of owners.

The entrances to both houses weren't very attractive, or practical. The steps up to Annette and Glen's front door were only two slabs wide, so that greeting friends meant everyone huddling together, or using the back door instead. So he created a much wider landing, using terracotta quarry tiles – not standard sized slabs – which were more in scale with the houses.

He also made the steps leading up to the Wrights' front door much wider so now they are shallow and gently curved, in the same brick as the house so that they blend in with it and the rest of the garden. (If money is tight, it's always worth tracking down the supplier of the bricks you want and seeing if they sell 'seconds'. These are obviously cheaper because they have some kind of superficial blemish but are just as strong as the first quality.) To give the entrance even more impact, and for reasons of safety, Rod put up a diagonal trellis, stained dark brown to match the woodwork on the house, closing off the side of the landing, and playing host to colourful climbers like evergreen ivy and the scented, yellow and crimson flowered honeysuckle *Lonicera × heckrottii*. The fact that the houses were on a slope from right to left meant that the Everitts only needed one step up to their front door, while the Wrights needed four. Once the new design was finished, the Everitts felt that their new entrance wasn't quite as imposing as next door's and so the design was amended to create a larger entrance area for them too.

The gardens sloped down towards the pavement, too, and while the slope could have been accommodated in the planting, Rod thinks a slight change of level makes a garden much more interesting visually, so he decided to put a low, curved brick wall across the two gardens, in the same bricks as the steps, to create an upper and lower level. Some of the soil excavated from the lower part of the garden to accommodate the stone chippings he planned to use, would be used to build up the upper level, behind the low retaining wall. Soil will eventually settle quite a bit, so if you don't build it right up to the top of the wall to start with, the plants that are meant to trail over the wall will disappear behind it and won't be seen at all.

Another big advantage in creating what is virtually a large raised bed, is that you create very good drainage, exactly what the sun-loving plants used in this garden need to do well.

With the slope taken care of, Rod turned his attention to the rest of the garden. He wanted something that was easy-care, but at the same time, something you could walk through, so on the lower level he chose to lay a very thin layer of chunky, cream Cotswold chippings – just under 2 cm (1 in) – on a good deep layer – at least 10 cm (4 in) – of consolidated sub-base. He stressed the importance of keeping those proportions right. If you skimp on the former and increase the depth of the latter, it makes it harder to walk on, and more inclined to ridge up.

By laying the chippings right to the edge of the drive, he also solved the problem of people getting muddy feet when they got out of the car. The concrete slab drive wasn't attractive, but since the budget didn't run to changing it at this stage, we planned to leave it till next year. The Wrights were so thrilled with the garden that they raised the money to re-do the drive with block paving to blend in.

As for the planting, Rod chose sun-loving plants that would largely take care of themselves, and give interest all year round – scented winter-flowering shrubs like *Daphne*

Top: The red berries of the cotoneaster and the bright yellow forsythia add welcome life and colour to what would otherwise be rather sterile front walls. *Above:* The bedding grown in containers outside this modern house have the same effect, though perhaps spraying the plastic urns a different colour would look even better.

odora 'Aureomarginata' and *Mahonia*, spring-flowering ones like *Viburnum* × *burkwoodii* 'Anne Russell', summer-flowering roses like the unusual, but very long-flowering, *R. chinensis* 'Mutabilis' and potentillas and autumn-flowering *Ceratostigma willmottianum*. There were also plenty of evergreens, particularly on the Everitts' side – *Cotoneaster salicifolius* 'Gnom' and the very small ornamental bramble, *Rubus calycinoides*.

Under the tree, he created an attractive circular bed, edged in brick, for shade-loving plants like *epimediums*, ivies, hellebores and autumn-flowering hardy *cyclamen*, together with a few ferns.

Although most of the planting is confined to the upper part of the garden, Rod has actually planted into the gravel as well, using tall, spiky plants like the elegant striped iris-like *Sisyrinchium striatum* with small pale yellow flowers, used as a recurring theme throughout the two gardens, as well as the white-flowered *Libertia grandiflora*.

Both couples were thrilled with the finished garden. As Annette said, 'We'll never move now!'

DOWN TO BASICS

Replacing a Lawn

You might be tempted, if you're planning to replace a lawn with a hard surface, just to leave it in place. However, if you pave over grass you eventually get a soggy, rotting layer of vegetation underneath which will not only smell vile, but which can destabilise the paving too. If you put gravel on top of grass or weeds, they will just grow through it.

So it is important to kill off the vegetation first, and perhaps the easiest and certainly the quickest way of doing that is to apply a weed-killer containing glyphosate (look for Tumbleweed or Round Up) when the grass and weeds are growing strongly – from mid-spring to late summer. In two or three weeks, the plants absorb the chemical right down to their roots and die off. Some other weedkillers only kill off the top growth so there's a chance that the more vigorous weeds will simply re-grow. Some really tough weeds like mare's tail and Japanese knotweed will grow again anyway, even after an application of glyphosate, so you will just have to keep on treating them whenever they appear.

Many organic gardeners are quite happy about using glyphosate because it becomes inactive immediately on contact with the soil, leaving no harmful residue. But if you really are determined to use no chemicals at all, the only answer is to cover the whole area with heavy grade black polythene or an old carpet, weight it down round the edges and leave it for a growing season. The total exclusion of light will kill off or terminally weaken almost everything.

Whatever method you use, once the weeds are completely dead, either scrape them off if you are going to hard-landscape the area, or dig them into the soil if you are going to re-plant it. It's all good organic matter which will improve the water-holding capacity and the fertility of your soil. As you dig over the soil in which you're going to plant, keep a sharp eye out for any pieces of root you come across and pull them out. Some weeds can re-grow from even a tiny piece of root left in the soil. Incidentally, it's not a good idea to cultivate too deeply any areas that you plan to hard-landscape. It will take the soil quite some time to compact again and if you put your paving down too soon you could have all sorts of problems as the soil settles.

Once the ground is cleared, this is the time to discover exactly what type of soil you're dealing with, because that will determine not only what sort of plants will thrive in it but also what you need to do to improve it. You need to know first of all whether it's acid or limey (alkaline); a simple-to-use lime testing kit from the garden centre costs about £1 and can save you a fortune in plants that sicken and die. Do take samples from several parts of the garden, incidentally. One area could be contaminated with builders' sand, for example, or cement and so give a false reading.

You also need to know the structure of the soil. If it's clay (it will stick together very easily to make a ball if it is) then, to make the soil easier to work and to prevent the roots of the plants rotting, you need to open it up and improve the drainage by digging in lots of coarse grit and organic matter – garden compost, well-rotted farmyard manure or composted straw. If you have the energy, double-digging a clay soil – which means digging down to two spades' depth – and working plenty of organic matter and grit into the lowest level, will pay dividends in years to come.

If the soil is sandy or chalky – you can't make it form a ball in your hand no matter how wet it is – then the problem is the opposite. Water drains away too quickly taking valuable nutrients with it so you need to improve its capacity for holding water by digging in lots of organic matter.

Although the organic matter will add nutrients, you also want to improve the soil's long-term fertility by digging in some slow release fertiliser as well. If you want to garden organically, then use hoof and horn (which will provide nitrogen) or seaweed or bone meal. Otherwise, a general fertiliser like Growmore would be fine.

Laying a gravel surface

As well as being one of the cheapest surfaces you can have, gravel is also very adaptable. It can look very formal, with low clipped box hedges, or very informal, with colourful plants growing through it and seeding themselves everywhere. It is also relatively easy to lay.

Go to your local builders' merchants (it's much cheaper to buy gravel there, incidentally, than at a garden centre) and have a look at what's on offer, for the colours can vary significantly. Gravel is literally the chip off the old block, and gravel from a limestone area will be quite different in colour to gravel from a sandstone area. If you have a choice, select the one that blends in best with the house.

Go for a large grade (¾ inch say) because it gives a more solid feel and doesn't stick to your shoes like the smaller stuff does. Smooth, washed gravel is slightly safer than spikier stone chippings if you have children. On the other hand, it is more attractive to the local cat population to use as a giant litter tray!

Before you lay gravel, you must first surround the area with some kind of edging to prevent it spreading everywhere. Obviously the house walls, or the garden walls would do the job on two or even three sides. On the other sides, you could use treated timber, a brick edging or a pre-cast concrete kerb.

Old railway sleepers make a good solid, relatively cheap edging if you can find them, though in a very small space they might be too bulky and look out of proportion with the rest of the garden.

If you've got clay or sandy soil or you plan to walk on it a lot, you'll need to spread a layer of whatever local sub-base material is easily available from the builders' merchants first, and compact it well with a heavy roller or a plate vibrator from the local hire shop. On top of that, spread 2 to 2.5 cm (just under an inch to 1 in) of gravel, and roll it in. You certainly don't want the gravel any deeper or it becomes difficult to walk through and ridges up.

To plant through gravel, initially, you'll need to make planting holes through the surface layer of gravel and the sub-base so that the roots of the plants can reach the soil below. After a few years, you'll find that soil works its way into the sub-base and the gravel, and you'll be able to plant directly into it.

PLANTS FOR GRAVEL

Many plants, particularly alpines, thrive in the good drainage that gravel provides. Most like a sunny spot but there are a few that will tolerate shade and that fact will be noted in each plant description.

Yarrow (*Achillea*)
Make sure you go for an alpine variety like 'King Edward' which has delicate ferny grey-green foliage and primrose yellow daisy-like flowers from June to September.
Height: 15 cm (6 in)

Bugle (*Ajuga reptans*)
All these useful carpeters are good for gravel. *A.r.* 'Variegata' will tolerate some shade. (See page 150.)

This row of modern pensioners' bungalows near Cambridge has deservedly
won prizes for its colourful front gardens.

Dryas × suendermannii
This evergreen spreading alpine has leathery dark green leaves and curious fluffy pale
cream flowers in early summer.
Height: 5 cm (2 in)

Alyssum saxatile
This is a perennial, not to be confused with its white annual relative. The most common
bright yellow variety is well known, but even nicer are the more subtle *A.s.* 'Compac-
tum' which has primrose yellow flowers from April to June, *A.s.* 'Dudley Neville' and
the larger *A.s.* 'Citrinum' which makes silvery mounds of foliage and has soft yellow
flowers.
Height: 15–25 cm (6–10 in)

Columbine *(Aquilegia)*
Again make sure you buy an alpine variety. *A. flabellata pumila* (or *akitensis*) has
attractive blue-green foliage and large blue and white flowers in late spring.
Height: 15 cm (6 in)

Anchusa caespitosa

An attractive evergreen with spiky dark green foliage and small, blue flowers in spring. It likes moist but free-draining soil.

Height: 2.5–5 cm (1–2 in)

Arabis ferdinandii-coburgii 'Variegata'

Its name is almost larger than it is! This plant forms low mounds of very attractive green and white variegated foliage and has white flowers in summer. Look too for *A. f-c.* 'Old Gold' which has golden variegated foliage and white flowers.

Height: 10 cm (4 in)

Thrift *(Armeria)*

Good very low-growing varieties of this evergreen cushion plant include *A. caespitosa* 'Bevan's Variety' which has bright pink flowers and deep green foliage and *A.c.* 'Alba' with white flowers. Both flower in May.

Slightly larger but still excellent is *A. maritima* 'Alba', which flowers from mid–late summer onwards.

Height: 6 cm (2–3 in)

Pieces of a glossy, man-made material make unusual crazy paving in this
suburban front garden.

Silver Mound (*Artemisia schmidtiana* 'Nana')
This beautiful delicate foliage plant forms silver mounds, hence its common American name. It does flower but the flowers are small and yellow and not very attractive, so snip the buds off and instead enjoy another flush of new bright silver foliage.
Height: 8cm (3in)

Aubrieta
One of the most widely grown alpines, usually in its purple form, and often paired with the acid yellow variety of *Alyssum saxatile*. There are other varieties in shades of pink, *A.* 'Maurice Prichard', of red, *A.* 'Red Carpet' and of lavender, *A.* 'Triumphant'. Prevent them from sprawling everywhere by cutting back hard after flowering, though if they do, and become bare in the centre, take cuttings from the healthy outer fringes. They are very easily grown from seed.
Height: 10cm (4in)

Bell flower (*Campanula*)
Again, make sure you buy an alpine variety, like any of the *C. carpatica* or *C. cochleariifolia* hybrids. See page 152.

Crepis incana
This has clear pink dandelion-like flowers for months in mid-summer and thrives in a well-drained sunny spot.
Height: 15–20cm (6–8in)

Alpine pinks (*Dianthus alpinus*)
These mat-forming plants have large, attractive flowers in shades of pink, red and white. Look out for *D.* 'Oakington' (warm rose pink), *D. deltoides* 'Brighteyes' (white flowers with a red 'eye') and *D.d.* 'Flashing Light' which have brilliant scarlet flowers. You can also grow it from seed.
Height: 5–15cm (2–6in)

Diascia 'Ruby Field'
A mat-forming perennial which bears masses of salmon pink flowers rather like those of *Nemesia* from mid-summer through to early autumn.
Height: 20cm (8in)

Dodecatheon meadia
This pretty plant, which sounds more like an Olympic event than an alpine, has pinky mauve flowers, not unlike a cyclamen, over clumps of smooth broad leaves. It's happiest in part-shade.
Height: 25cm (10in)

128

Draba aizoides

Other members of the family are best grown in the protection of an alpine house, but given the very good drainage that gravel provides, this one should be all right outside. It has rosettes of stiff leaves and bright golden yellow flowers in early spring.

Height: 8cm (3in)

Fleabane *(Erigeron mucronatus or karvinskianus)*

This lax, spreading perennial has masses of daisy-like flowers which open white, then turn to pink and purple as they age, giving a tri-colour effect. It looks wonderful growing between slabs or in walls.

Height: 10–15cm (4–6in)

Gentian *(Gentiana septemfida latifolia)*

Although the autumn-flowering gentians need a lime-free soil, this mid- to late-summer-flowering one will flower in any rich, reasonably well-drained soil.

Height: 15cm (6in)

Crane's-bill *(Geranium)*

Among the best alpine varieties are *G. cinereum* 'Ballerina', with lilac-pink flowers veined with red and *G. subcaulescens*, with crimson flowers from May to July, G. 'Laurence Flatman' with soft, mauve pink flowers mottled with magenta from May to September.

Height: 10–15cm (4–6in)

Helianthemum

These are wonderful evergreen dwarf shrubs for any sunny spot in well-drained soil, whether cascading over a wall or rock, or as ground-cover. They come in a whole range of colours, from pure white with soft grey foliage ('The Bride') through yellow ('Jubilee'), apricot ('Amy Baring'), orange ('Henfield Brilliant'), red ('Fireball' or 'Mrs Earle') to pink ('Annabel' or 'Wisley Pink') and even bi-colour ('Raspberry Ripple'). Clip them over with the shears after flowering if they start getting untidy.

Height: 25cm (10in)

Hypericum olympicum

This dense rounded dwarf shrub is smothered in large bright yellow flowers throughout summer. *H.o.* 'Citrinum' has beautiful soft yellow flowers.

Height: 30cm (12in)

Iberis 'Little Gem'

This smaller-growing relative of the old favourite 'Snowflake' forms a mound of deep evergreen foliage smothered in pure white flowers in early summer.

Height: 15cm (6in)

A dramatic transformation in our communal new estate garden after less than three months. The enlarged steps and serpentine wall across the centre gives it very strong 'bones', although the planting is already softening the hard landscaping.

Lewisia

These beautiful clump-forming alpines have a reputation for being difficult because they are liable to rot in wet weather. The answer is to grow them vertically, between two rocks so that water can't settle in the rosette of leaves and start the rotting process. They like part-shade.

Height: 30 cm (12 in)

Dwarf flax (*Linum flavum* 'Compactum')

In a sunny sheltered position and protected from winter wet, this dwarf flax will produce masses of funnel-shaped yellow flowers in summer.

Height: 30 cm (12 in)

Lithospermum diffusum (or Lithodora diffusa) 'Heavenly Blue'

If you have an acid soil, do try this for its abundance of deep blue flowers. *L.d.* 'Grace Ward' has slightly larger flowers of a more intense shade of blue. It blooms from June to October.

Height: 15 cm (6 in)

Mimulus 'Andean Nymph'
This dwarf monkey flower has masses of pretty rose pink and creamy yellow flowers, a bit like a cross between a snapdragon and a foxglove.
Height: 15 cm (6 in)

White Cup *(Nierembergia rivularis)*
A succession of white, inverted bell-shaped flowers are carried above a mat of bright green foliage from June to September.
Height: 5 cm (2 in)

Oxalis adenophylla
Some members of the family are real garden thugs but this one, with its beautiful soft grey-green leaves and pinky-mauve flowers in spring, is very well-behaved.
Height: 5 cm (2 in)

Penstemon pinifolius
An evergreen bushy plant which has masses of tubular orange-red flowers from mid to late summer onwards.
Height: 15 cm (6 in)

Phlox subulata and *douglasii*
Both are mat-forming, free-flowering alpines in a range of colours from pure white to blue and bright red which flower in early summer. Good ones to look for include *P.s.* 'Bonita' (lavender with a darker blue eye), 'Oakington Blue' (sky blue), 'White Delight' and 'Scarlet Flame'. Among the *P.d.* hybrids 'Rose Cushion' (rose pink), 'May Snow' and 'Waterloo' (rich crimson) are all good.
Height: 10–15 cm (4–6 in)

Pasque Flower *(Pulsatilla vulgaris)*
With its pretty ferny foliage and violet mauve flowers (there is white form, too, *P.v.* 'Alba'), this makes a pretty contribution to the spring garden.
Height: 20 cm (8 in)

Saxifrage *(Saxifraga)*
There are lots of excellent varieties with flowers in shades of red, pink, yellow and white to choose from. Buy them in flower from the garden centre so you know just what you're getting.
Height: 10–15 cm (4–6 in)

Stonecrop *(Sedum)*
Again, there's a wide choice on offer. See page 156.

Houseleeks (*Sempervivum*)

People become addicted to these and build up huge collections. Their rosettes of fleshy leaves in a range of colours are very striking, as are their spikes of flowers in June–July.
Height: 10–15 cm (4–6 in)

Double sea campion (*Silene maritima* 'Flore Pleno')

This perennial with spiky green-grey leaves has white pompom-like flowers in summer.
Height: 20 cm (8 in)

Sisyrinchium striatum

The iris-like leaves of this semi-evergreen perennial, with spikes of small creamy yellow flowers in summer, is a useful contrast in shape to many of the rounded hummock-forming alpines. *S.s.* 'Aunt May' or 'Variegata' (or *Phaiophleps* 'Aunt May' or 'Variegata' as the botanists now say we should call it. We would if we could!) has pale grey green and cream striped leaves. Much smaller is *S. bellum* with green grass-like foliage and blue flowers from mid-summer to autumn.
Height: 12–45 cm (5–18 in)

Thyme (*Thymus*)

There are lots of low-growing varieties to choose from – *T.* 'Doone Valley' with dark green and gold variegated foliage and mauve flowers, *T. serpyllum* 'Annie Hall' with shell-pink flowers and *T.s.* 'Albus' with white flowers.
Height: 8 cm (2–3 in)

Veronica prostrata 'Trehane' or 'Blue Sheen'

This low-growing perennial forms mats of fresh green foliage above which are carried spikes of vivid blue flowers ('Trehane') or wisteria blue ('Blue Sheen') in early summer.
Height: 15 cm (6 in)

Viola

This family of lovely old favourites includes the dramatic 'Bowles Black', the larger flowered but less free-flowering 'Penny Black', the delightful creamy yellow 'Moonlight' (looks wonderful grown with either of the black-flowered ones) and the pale blue 'Maggie Mott' and 'Norah Leigh'. The horned violas *V. cornuta* are also well worth growing for their masses of smaller flowers in white, china blue or purple.

California fuchsia (*Zauschneria californica* 'Glasnevin')

This very showy plant has masses of tubular deep orange-scarlet flowers in late summer and autumn. It's not reliably hardy in colder areas, but should survive in a sheltered sunny spot – at the base of a wall for instance. The slightly smaller *Z.c. microphylla* has greyer leaves and scarlet flowers and can withstand extreme drought.
Height: 30–38 cm (12–15 in)

CHAPTER SEVEN

THE SLOPING GARDEN

*M*any gardens slope to a greater or lesser degree, usually up to the house from the street, but sometimes they slope down to the house and this can create problems with drainage.

The sloping garden we chose, in front of the detached 1950s bungalow belonging to Paul and Gill Wallis, not only sloped up moderately steeply from the pavement to the front door, it also sloped down, from right to left, though fortunately a little more gently this time.

The usual advice on coping with a sloping back garden is to terrace it but if the front garden also has to accommodate cars, as this one and so many others must, then it isn't that simple. Unless you've always fancied being a stunt driver, and enjoy driving up and down steps, then you must have a smooth incline for the driveway and parking area. If you terrace the rest of the garden, you have to make sure that one area joins another in a practical and visually satisfying way.

The Wallises' front garden, which measures approximately 13m wide × 6m deep (42 × 20ft) and faces north-north-east, also demonstrates very graphically the problems of incorporating cars into a front garden. They have three cars to cope with, belonging to Paul, Gill and their daughter, Sue, and only one garage. Sue is moving out soon, but they are a sociable couple with plenty of visitors and while it is possible to park on the road – there are no yellow lines – there is quite a lot of fast through-traffic and they feel happier with off-street parking.

As with the Wallises, where a household has three or four cars, it's usually because there are young adults in the family, who will sooner or later move on to homes of their own. It seems a pity, therefore, to turn the front garden into a car park permanently. One relatively temporary solution would be to lay Monoslab grass/concrete units on an area of lawn. These are blocks studded with small, flat-topped concrete pyramids between which, once laid, you spread top soil and grass seed so that they blend in with the lawn. Once you no longer need so much parking space you can remove them, fill in with soil and reseed.

As things stood, the Wallises did have ample parking space for the cars but the vast expanse of tarmac, which was not in very good condition anyway, dominated the front garden. Also as it was right up to the walls, it did nothing to show the bungalow off to its best advantage.

Apart from that, on the right of the drive, there was a very small patch of scrubby lawn containing just one very sorry-looking cherry tree, which hadn't taken kindly to a very recent radical prune, and a narrow bed of lily-of-the-valley all round the base of the wall.

The main part of the garden, on the other side of the tarmac, sloped very gently from the house down to a low stone retaining wall about 45 cm (18 in) high. Just behind the wall was a scalloped flowerbed (Paul's unsuccessful attempt to stop the postman hopping up and creating his own 'desire line' across the lawn and the flowerbeds to the front door), then a small patch of lawn and an informal pond, situated just below the bedroom window, hidden away behind large stones. When we first saw the garden, there were some colourful spring- and summer-flowering plants – aubrieta, arabis, delphiniums, hardy geraniums, a hybrid tea rose or two, a broom, which had self-seeded from the back garden, and a young *Magnolia stellata*.

Paul and Gill were both enthusiastic gardeners and, having created all sorts of interesting features in the back garden, really wanted to do something as interesting with the front. But they'd had to admit defeat. They just didn't know where to start.

What they did know was how much they want to keep of the existing garden. They loved looking out onto the pond from the bedroom window and, on a purely practical level, Gill also wanted some kind of level area right next to the house, so that she could clean the windows easily.

They also wanted to keep some of the plants – the *Magnolia stellata*, for instance, which was a present. If it didn't fit into the new plan for the front garden, they were quite happy to move it to the back. Although it was really too late to move it, Paul dug it up with a very large rootball and put it into a pot, and so far, seems to have got away with it!

Moving some of the choicer perennials wasn't a problem. In an ideal world you wouldn't choose to move plants like delphiniums which are just about to flower, but since the work had to start, the choice was either to dig them up and throw them on the compost heap, or move them and hope for the best. We prepared their new planting hole in the back garden, gave them a thorough watering, then dug them up and replanted them immediately with a sprinkling of rose fertiliser and another bucketful of water. Fortunately, they survived!

The Wallises were also clear about what they did *not* want to keep. The tarmac could certainly go – they had already budgeted to replace that with something more attractive – and they didn't want so much hardstanding. The lawn could go, too: it was too small, Paul reckoned, to justify the effort involved. And as for the flowering cherry, although once a lovely tree, it was now beyond salvation and would have to come out.

The fact that the Wallises had some fairly strong likes and dislikes, even though they were unclear about the overall look of the garden, meant that Susannah Brown, one of our brightest young designers, had something to get her teeth into.

The design Susannah came up with solved the problems of too much tarmac and of the two-dimensional slope very well. Basically, she pivoted the whole axis of the garden through 45°, so that the drive became a Y shape, then created lines of terraces and a new triangular front step to run parallel with the left hand arm of the Y.

She kept the entrance to the drive the same width and then broadened it out higher up into an area that was smaller than the existing hardstanding but still wide enough to turn a car round or park an extra car. Paul marked out the lines of the new drive on the old one with chalk and drove in and out to make sure he still had ample room to manoeuvre.

They chose 'brindle' Driveline 50 blocks, a product designed specially for DIY, laid in a herringbone pattern for strength as well as looks, to replace the tarmac. This was a vast improvement but, even so, in order to reduce the area they covered still further and to play down the 'bricky' look, Susannah replaced the blocks on the left arm of the Y between the end of the garage and the new front step with the same slabs and gravel she used in the garden itself. Since they were set on the same strong sub-base as the blocks, the area still provided parking for a third car but now looked like part of the garden, rather than yet more hardstanding.

Susannah terraced the rest of the garden using wooden sleepers to retain the soil, following the 45° line of the Y, with the occasional zigzag at 90° to cope with the widthways slope. She had initially thought of using large chunks of stone to retain the soil but decided this look was too informal for such a formal setting and that wooden sleepers, although organic, would give the garden a little more formality with their solid, straight lines. They were considerably cheaper, too, as well as being easier to handle and to lay well.

She covered the terraced area with gravel, using strategically placed stepping stones under the windows for Gill's window cleaning and, working on the principle of 'If you can't beat 'em, join 'em' principle, also incorporated stepping-stones for the postman along his already well-established 'desire line' across the garden!

To accommodate the Wallises' love of water, Susannah created two small, formal pools on different levels, with the water trickling down from one to the other and a concealed pump to pump it back up to the top again. Since water running continually over wood

Before, (*top*) the bungalow's garden was neat but uninspiring. Seen from down the hill, the new railway sleeper terracing makes a dramatic difference.

would eventually encourage rotting, we put a piece of slate over the sleeper at that point to protect it.

Right up against the house, Susannah has created two beds to soften the rather stark brick walls: a triangular one in the corner between the garage and the front wall and, to the left of the front door, a low narrow rectangular one.

As for the planting, Susannah wanted plants that would cope with a somewhat exposed north-facing site, although because it was so open, it got a lot of sun in the summer. Some plants would have to cope with dryish gravel while others would be placed around the pools. What's more, they would all have to work together in a satisfying whole. She chose a number of evergreen foliage plants for all-year-round interest, including shrubs with good, strong, vertical lines to balance the strong horizontal lines of the hard landscaping and the sleepers, like the spiky evergreen mahonia, *M.* × 'Charity', the even spikier *Yucca gloriosa*, the latter planted well away from where children might venture, variegated ivies and *Chamaecyparis lawsoniana* 'Columnaris Glauca', although, obviously, it would be a few years before they were large enough to do the job properly.

There were also low-growing evergreens, like *Prunus laurocerasus* 'Otto Luyken', the tall, narrow yew, *Taxus baccata* 'Fastigiata', and the Japanese cedar, *Cryptomeria japonica* 'Nana', to grow over the terraces and soften the lines of the sleepers.

She included deciduous shrubs too, such as berberis with gold and wine-red foliage and the lovely golden cut-leafed elder (*Sambucus racemosa* 'Plumosa Aurea'). To add maturity to a newly planted garden, Susannah believes it's well worth splashing out on a few larger, more mature plants. Certainly £25 on a large *Rhus glabra* 'Laciniata' was money well spent.

Some of the herbaceous plants like hostas, artemisia and *Heuchera* 'Palace Purple' and grasses like the steel blue *Festuca glauca* were chosen for their foliage. But that's not to say there isn't plenty of flower colour, too, for example in the bright orange of *Potentilla* 'Orange Star', the touch of white in the hardy evergreen cistus (*C.* × *corbariensis*), forming an informal hedge along the postman's path, and the blue *Iris sibirica* by the pool.

Up against the shady walls of the bungalow Susannah has chosen to grow the small-leafed variegated ivy 'Goldheart' and on the garage and the wall opposite, she planted the climbing rose 'Maigold' with its lovely bronze-gold semi double blooms.

Her choice of primarily warm colours, like the orange and yellow of the flowers and the matching yellow of the foliage, was to warm up the hard materials; and since these work well with both orange-red brick and the cooler buff paving and gravel they help give the garden its unity.

From the first day the garden was planted, the Wallises loved it. Paul's favourite vantage point was sitting on the front step of the bungalow, looking down across the garden, and they were already planning on what they might add to it in future years.

Coping with a slope

If your front garden only slopes gently away from the house, you could plant it with ground-cover plants which, once established, will hold the soil in place with their roots and prevent 'land creep'. It's probably best to choose a fair proportion of evergreens to give you something attractive to look at all year round, like low-growing cotoneaster, *C. salicifolius* or *C. horizontalis*, variegated euonymus, winter-flowering heathers, ivies and the hardy geraniums, *G. macrorrhizum* 'Album' or 'Walter Ingwersen', which are virtually evergreen, or the low-growing bistort or knotweed (*Persicaria* which used to be called 'Polygonum' until very recently) *P. affine* 'Dimity', or 'Superba' which, while not evergreen, will keep its attractive, dead, russet-coloured leaves until the new growth starts in the spring. You will also need some taller plants to add visual interest, such as a slender dwarf conifer, like *Juniperus communis* 'Sentinel', the very slender golden yew *Taxus baccata* 'Standishii', or the purple-leafed berberis *B. thunbergii* 'Helmond Pillar'.

On a slightly steeper bank, in the short term, it's a good idea to cover the area with netting pegged down at the edges which will hold the soil in place, and then to plant through holes cut in it. These days, it's hard to find anything but plastic netting which, of course, won't rot down, but as long as you are prepared to make the holes larger and larger as the plants start to spread and to cut it away altogether once they are established, it will do the trick.

Simply planting the slope is fine if you are dealing with a reasonably gentle gradient but for steeper slopes, terracing and retaining walls are really the only answer.

Terracing involves a technique called 'cut and fill' which means cutting into the slope at right angles to create a series of large steps and taking the soil you've dug out from the top half of the slope and using it to fill the bottom half. To keep the soil in place, even if the change of level is only a foot or so, you will need to build a retaining wall, otherwise the exposed vertical face of the soil will quickly start to crumble.

Obviously, since retaining walls hold back large quantities of soil which is very heavy, especially when it's wet, they must be strongly built. You can use wood (provided it is treated to prevent rotting), brick, or natural stone if you can get it, or pre-cast concrete walling blocks, of which there is now a wide range available aimed at the DIY market.

When you start terracing, you must first of all take off the top soil to at least a spade's depth and put that somewhere until the levelling is finished. You can then put it back in the beds you will be creating or use it somewhere else in the garden. Whatever you do, don't dump it or give it away otherwise, once you've made your terraces, you'll be left with only subsoil, and trying to grow plants in that is a thankless task.

If you're good at DIY, you should be able to tackle walls of up to 1.2m (4ft) in height. For anything higher than that, or if you are planning to use the area above the retaining wall for parking cars, you should call in a professional. You will need to put in good solid foundations. For a wall 1.2m (4ft) high they need to be three times the width of the wall and 50cm (20in) deep to allow for 15cm (6in) of concrete plus a couple of courses of blocks or bricks below soil level.

It is absolutely essential, whatever material you use, to include 'weepholes' for drainage. If you don't, the weight of water trapped behind the wall can build up to such an extent that it could push the wall over. If you are using bricks, just leave a gap of 50mm (2in) every three feet or so on the bottom course of bricks. Or you could use lengths of pipe about 50mm (2in) in diameter, and the depth of the wall plus 30cm (12in) in length. Position them so they are flush with the wall at the front and sticking into the soil behind. Earthenware pipes look decorative but plastic will do the job just as well.

Don't forget that the water from the weepholes has to go somewhere, but if you have beds at the base of the wall you can grow plants that enjoy fairly moist soil.

The walls themselves offer you a marvellous opportunity to grow a whole range of plants to trail down or climb up them, or even to grow between the stones. Many rock plants should do well. Think of mats of aubrieta, not just the common mauve, but reds, pinks and lavender blues as well, tumbling over the top of the wall. Also try *Alyssum saxatile*, though for my taste a soft yellow like *A.s.* 'Dudley Neville' is preferable to the usual bright yellow type that's usually grown with purple aubrieta. For later on in the year, try campanulas which are smothered in white or blue flowers for weeks on end.

If your walls get sun most of the day, rock roses (*helianthemum*) are hard to beat. They come in a range of colours from white through pale yellow and pink to the most vivid deep orange (see page 129) and again flower all summer long. *Saxifraga*, *sedum* and *sempervivum* (houseleeks) will thrive in crevices in walls.

If your front garden slopes down to the house, you will have more opportunity to enjoy it from indoors. But of course a garden that slopes that way does create more potentially serious problems with drainage, because all the water will come trickling down the garden and, if you do nothing about it, could eventually seep into the foundations.

What you must do, therefore, is make a good wide flat area at ground level to push the soil well back from the house, and install a proper drainage system underneath it. At the base of the retaining wall, where the weepholes are, you need to make a gully sloping gently to a drain so that the water is taken away at once and doesn't lie in puddles.

With a small front garden, it's probably best to make your first terrace as wide as possible and then two or three much narrower terraces further away from the house. It will give you a greater sense of space and won't feel as claustrophobic as steep retaining walls closer to the house.

The water in the two formal pools provides a smooth, reflective surface in
contrast to the rough texture of the gravel and the wood.

Driveways

The choice of hard surfacing for a front garden is more important in many ways than the choice for the back garden, particularly if you have a driveway, because there will be an awful lot of it. So it has to look as attractive as possible and blend in with the house too.

There are also practical considerations to bear in mind. You want a surface that will not be slippery when wet and will withstand a lot of wear and tear. And since cars are going to be driven across it, it must be laid on good solid foundations to take the weight.

There are a number of factors to be borne in mind when planning a driveway. It has to be wide enough to allow car doors to open on both sides without either banging into a wall, or forcing visitors to step straight on to the lawn or into a flowerbed – on average, about 3m (10ft). And if it also doubles as the path it must be wide enough to allow people like the milkman and dustman to get past the car with crates or dustbins without scratching the paintwork. One space-saving solution, if you have a longish driveway, is to keep the approach narrow and widen it out only in the stopping or parking area.

Bear in mind obstacles such as gate posts, low walls or even the front step. Make sure access is as straightforward and as risk-free as possible, both driving in *and* reversing out.

If you live on a busy main road where it just isn't safe to reverse out, then you'll need a turning area for the car. Although you could probably work out on paper how large it needs to be for your car, it's probably safest to find a large open space somewhere – a deserted car park on a Sunday, say. With the help of a friend, some strategically placed plastic bottles or cardboard cartons and a large tape measure, find out exactly what is the minimum area you need to manoeuvre. You may feel a bit silly doing it, but you'd feel even sillier if you went ahead and laid the drive and then found you couldn't manoeuvre without driving into your new flowerbeds!

It also pays to think ahead. You may be driving a Mini now but in a few years' time it could be an estate car, so increase the area you need at present to allow for expansion! And of course if you want to sell your house, a would-be buyer could have a much bigger car than yours.

If you have any choice in the matter, don't put the turning area directly in front of the house. A wide area of paving or tarmac right outside the front door always looks rather sterile and unwelcoming, as the Wallises' bungalow demonstrated only too clearly. If you have to put it there, try and leave space for some narrow beds right next to the house so that you can at least put some greenery between hard surface and house walls, as Susannah Brown has done. It might be possible to put the turning area right inside the front gate and then create a border between it and the house.

If you are creating a completely new driveway, you should check with the local planning authority first whether or not you need planning permission. And whether you're working on a new driveway, or renovating an existing one, always contact the local electricity and gas boards, the water authority and BT and ask for copy plans to see whether any services are directly under the drive and at what depth. In most cases, they are at least 18 inches below the surface – 2 feet in new houses, but better to be safe than sorry.

You may find you have an inspection cover right in the middle of the driveway and if you are laying a new surface on top of the old one this will need to be re-set to the new level. To minimise the visual impact, you can get special inspection covers, designed to take blocks or paving to match the surrounding area, so that all you see is a narrow metal rim. These covers are totally safe, incidentally, and just as strong as the ordinary ones.

Surfaces

There is a wide range of different surfaces available, and while some need to be professionally laid, there are others that can be laid by an averagely competent DIY'er. The choice depends primarily on your budget. After that, it's a question of personal taste, though obviously a surface that tones with the bricks of the house will look better than one that clashes, and it's worth bearing scale in mind too. In a small area, small blocks, bricks or slabs look much better than large ones.

BRICKS OR BLOCKS

Paving blocks, which look like bricks when laid, are widely used in public areas like forecourts and car parks but are available in an increasingly wide range of attractive colours for domestic situations. (A dark 'brindle' or mottled colour, incidentally, will hide oil stains much better than a pale, plain one.)

They are made from very dense concrete, which gives them their extremely hard-wearing properties, and since they are bedded on to sand rather than cement or mortar, on top of a well-compacted sub-base for strength, they are relatively easy to lay.

With the introduction of new slimline blocks like Driveline 50 (50mm thick as opposed to the standard 80mm) it will be possible in many cases to lay them on the existing drive, provided it is sound and provided that, when laid, they are still 15cm (6in) below the damp proof course. Remember that, with the sand on which they are bedded, they will add a total 10cm (4in) to existing levels.

If the new level would be too close to the DPC or if the drive is in a very poor state, or if you are starting on virgin soil, you will need to lay a sub-base first. What you will need, apart from the blocks, is material for the sub-base – crushed stone, quarry waste or hoggin, depending on what's most readily available locally – and a supply of sharp sand (*not* soft builders' sand). The builders' merchant or garden centre which supplies the blocks will be able to tell you the quantities you need once they know the area to be paved. You will also need to hire a plate vibrator, and unless you are very lucky and find that the blocks fill the area exactly, a block cutter. You should have no difficulty in hiring both from the local hire shop.

Start by marking out the area of the drive with pegs and string. Life will be made a whole lot easier if you can make it an exact number of blocks wide. Since the strongest bond for heavy duty areas is herringbone (and it looks most interesting too) it might be simplest to lay a couple of rows out on the ground in the correct pattern and measure that.

If you're not using the old drive as a sub-base, then dig out the soil to the required depth: 10cm (4in) of sub-base if the drive is to take just the weight of a family car (up to twice that depth for anything heavier, like an oil delivery lorry); plus 5cm (2in) of compacted sand (you actually put on a layer 6.5cm (2½in) deep to allow for compaction to the right level); plus the depth of the block – either 5, 6.5 or 8cm.

Cut some wooden pegs (they should be the total depth plus 15cm (6in) for hammering into the soil) and hammer them in to the ground about 1m apart, until they are at the same level as the surrounding area and at the level the finished drive will be. Make sure they are level in every direction by putting a straight edge (a long timber batten for example) between each peg and its neighbours in turn, and checking with a spirit level.

You will need to allow for a slight 'fall' – about 1 in 50 – to carry rainwater off the surface of the drive and into the adjoining flowerbeds or lawn. To set a fall on either side of a drive 2.5m wide, cut a small piece of timber 2.5cm in length. Place it on top of the peg closest to the edge and then hammer the peg down until the spirit level placed on a straight piece of wood between that peg, plus the 2.5cm of timber, and the peg in the centre of the drive (a distance of 1.25m), is exactly level. When you remove the straight edge, and the 2.5cm piece of timber, the outside peg will be exactly 2.5cm below the centre peg, giving you the 1 in 50 'fall' that you need. Repeat on the other side.

Next mark the pegs at 10cm (4in) above the soil – or the correct depth for the sub-base you're going to lay – and make another mark 6.5cm above that, which is the level of the sand. Don't panic, incidentally, if you then add the depth of your block and find the remaining bit of the peg appears to be 1.5cm short. You haven't made a mistake. Once

In this small suburban garden, the design in cobbles in the same colour as
the crazy paving makes an interesting contrast in texture, while its curves are
reflected in the sweep of white alyssum.

the blocks are laid and have been vibrated they will settle 1.5 cm and so the drive will
finish up at the right level.

Lay the sub-base and compact it to the right level. When that's done, or if you are
using an existing drive as a base, you will need to fix the edging to keep the sand and the
blocks in place. If you're paving right up to the house or a garden wall, then the walls are
a perfectly good edging.

On an edge adjoining a lawn or flowerbeds there are several options. You could use a
preformed concrete kerb which is bedded into mortar, and 'haunched' (held in place
with a cement fillet behind it) either to stand proud of the paving or to be level with it. Or
you can use timber, again held in place with a fillet of cement, though in time the timber
will rot. Straight lines present no problems and neither, really, do curves. You can either
use a 'small element curb system' (small pieces of curbing which can be made to form a
gentle curve) or you can use flexible timber bent to shape and nailed at regular intervals
to pegs, and held in place by a fillet of concrete.

With all these methods, you must wait a few days until the cement has set completely
before you can finish laying the blocks. If you don't want to wait, you could use
Keyform, a special polymer triangular edging tube which can be used on straight edges
or sawn part-through at intervals to allow it to curve. You simply fix it in place with long
steel nails hammered into the ground but, again, do check first that there are no services

like electricity, gas or water mains just below the surface! The blocks can be laid immediately and once the drive is finished, the edging is invisible.

Once your edging is firmly in place, you'll need two long battens 6.5cm deep, and a straight-edged plank a metre or so long. Place the two battens parallel on the sub-base, less than a metre apart, and spread the sand over the surface as evenly as you can, roughly level with the mark on the pegs so that it's just slightly above the battens. Then resting the plank on the battens, pull it towards you dragging the surplus away so that the sand left behind is now smooth and level with the battens – exactly 6.5cm deep. Move the battens and repeat until you have levelled the whole area. Obviously you must avoid walking on the sand you've levelled, so start up against one firm edge and work backwards.

Start laying the blocks in the herringbone pattern, and butt them up against each other as tightly as you can. The design of each block means there will be enough space for the sand to work its way between them and lock them together. If you need to stand on the blocks as you work – and obviously on a wide expanse of driveway you will – then use a plank to spread the weight and keep as far away as you can from the last couple of rows laid because you could inadvertently move them out of position.

When the blocks have been laid, and any part-blocks cut to fit, go over the surface with the plate vibrator at least two or three times until the surface is at the level it should be. When it is, scatter the special fine sand over the surface, brush it in and then vibrate the whole surface again a couple of times. And that's it.

It's just as easy to lay a gently sloping drive this way, too, providing you make sure that the slope is straight and doesn't dip in the middle, which could cause the car to 'bottom' (hit its lower parts like the sump) where the slope meets the level parking area at the top, or hit the exhaust where the slope joins the level roadway. Make sure, too, that there is a really firm edging across the bottom of the slope and work upwards from there.

It's hard work physically, but two reasonably fit people should be able to lay an average sized driveway in a long weekend.

CONCRETE

You can make a drive from poured concrete, which is one of the cheaper methods. You will need to make a timber framework in which to pour the concrete, so that you can get it absolutely level and give it a good firm edge. You also need to leave small gaps between large areas of concrete to allow for expansion, otherwise it will crack.

The ideal size for each section is one that allows you time to pour the concrete, tamp it level and give it a surface before it sets, which is about two hours. You can give the concrete a completely smooth finish but a textured surface won't be slippery in wet weather, so either leave the final tamping ridges, or lightly brush the surface, always in the same direction, with a stiff broom. For a brushed aggregate finish, which just exposes the small round pebbles used in the concrete and gives a more interesting textured finish, make sure you use the right mix to start with and then, just before the concrete sets, brush it with a stiff broom to remove the top layer of cement and expose the aggregate.

Newly laid concrete will need protection from the weather – whether rain, hot sun or drying winds – so cover it with polythene and leave it for at least three days. While you can walk on it after 48 hours, it won't reach its full strength for 28 days and so you avoid driving a car onto it for as long as possible.

One solution to the problem of oil drips on a concrete drive is to make a shallow gully a couple of feet wide down the centre and fill it with gravel, or pebbles which can be raked over or replaced if they get very badly stained.

There are specialist firms which lay paths and drives using impressed concrete, in which templates are pressed into nearly-set concrete, coloured in a range of shades, to produce the desired finish – bricks, setts, crazy paving, and so on. At the time of writing these aren't available for DIY use, though it's always worth enquiring if the idea appeals.

GRAVEL

This is certainly one of the cheaper surfaces, but gravel drives look best when sweeping up to very substantial country or suburban houses, and are not really suitable for drives in small urban gardens. However if you do want gravel, then it will need edging to stop it spreading everywhere. Start with a good layer of hard-core which has been well-compacted – at least 10 cm (4 in) or up to twice that depth if it's to take a lot of weight – then 6 cm (2½ in) of binding gravel, sometimes called 'as dug', also well consolidated (it is unwashed, so the clay left in it hardens and binds it together) and finally lay on 5 cm (2 in) coarse gravel or pea shingle – the rounded stones are much less sharp than stone chippings. Firm the whole area with a heavy roller and water it. This will get the binding gravel doing its job.

PAVING SLABS

Unless you have a small drive – or a very large bank balance – York stone will be out of the question. And besides it seems almost an act of vandalism to allow engine oil to stain its beautiful surface! But the imitation pre-cast concrete slabs now on the market at a fraction of the price look so good that it's no great sacrifice. There is such a very wide range of shapes, colours and textures available that you are almost spoilt for choice and it ought to be relatively easy to choose something that blends with the house. While it's advisable to stick to just one colour (a checkerboard of rhubarb- and custard-coloured slabs is not exactly restful!) there's no reason why you can't create a more interesting-looking surface by using slabs of different shapes and sizes – in scale with the house – from the same range, or by breaking up an expanse of plain rectangular slabs with an occasional square of bricks or cobbles (ideal as an oil drip trap anyway, at the point where the car usually stands).

To support the weight of the car, the slabs need to be laid on a concrete base. The preparation is the same as for laying blocks except that instead of sand you will lay a 5cm (2in) layer of mortar: one part cement to four part sharp sand, mixed fairly dry, on top of the sub-base. If it's too wet, the slabs will simply sink into it.

Level the mortar as you would for concrete, and then set the first slab in place, tapping it down with the handle of a hammer until it's at the correct level. Use a spirit level to check in each direction. It's absolutely vital to get this one right – if it is even slightly out of true then the rest of the drive will be catastrophically so.

When it is level, lay the next slab using that one as a guide. Since mortar dries out in a couple of hours, work on a fairly small area at a time. Ideally, it's a job for two – one of you can be mixing up and levelling the mortar, while the other one lays the slabs.

TARMAC

This is another reasonably cheap option for a driveway but, it has to be said, probably the least attractive. The dark charcoal grey surface, especially if scattered with white chips, does nothing for any house and the coloured versions are little better. The other problem is that it has gained a bad reputation because of the many cowboys who are in the business of laying it. Remember those Boys from the Blackstuff in the 1980s television series? So if tarmac's what you want, don't give the job to a couple of blokes who knock on the door and ask if you want a new drive put in that very day. Get a professional firm to lay it, and make sure that they are putting in an adequate sub-base to take the weight of a car. You also need to make sure that they put in a proper edging of brick or concrete – otherwise the frost will simply crumble the edge of the tarmac away. You could make it look better by asking them to roll gravel or pea shingle, toning with your house, into the surface before it sets.

GROUND-COVER PLANTS

For a sloping garden, and indeed for low-maintenance gardens, ground-cover plants are ideal because they quickly cover the soil, holding it in place with their roots, and they look very attractive too. There are a number of excellent ground-cover shrubs, like the cotoneasters and junipers that Susannah Brown has used in the Wallises' garden. A number of them are listed on page 110 including the ground-hugging *Ceanothus thyrsiflorus* 'Repens' or 'Blue Mound', *Euonymus fortunei*, *Hebe*, ground-cover roses, Christmas box (*Sarcococca humilis*) and periwinkle (*Vinca minor*).

Below is a list of excellent ground-covering perennials; the 'plants per square metre' is the number required to cover that amount of ground in two or three years.

Bugle (*Ajuga reptans*)
The red and purple-leafed forms are excellent carpeters for a sunny border. Good varieties include *A. metallica* which has dark purple, crinkly leaves, 'Braunherz' whose purple leaves have a bronze sheen, and 'Burgundy Glow' which has wine-red leaves. For a shady spot, the cream and green variegated bugle *A.r.* 'Variegata' is ideal. They all have spikes of deep blue flowers.
Height: 10 cm (4 in). Plants per square metre: 7.

Lady's mantle (*Alchemilla mollis*)
Its fresh green leaves look like carefully folded fans as they open, and it carries sprays of tiny yellow-green flowers for months on end in summer. It will grow practically anywhere – sun or shade, damp or dry soil, acid or alkaline – and seeds itself with alacrity in the crevices of paving, in walls, or on steps. Just pull it out where you don't want it.
Height: 50 cm (18 in). Plants per square metre: 5.

Japanese anemones (*Anemone japonica*)
These not only provide welcome late summer/early autumn colour with their masses of tall pink or white flowering stems which need no staking, but they also spread to form large clumps of foliage. Good varieties to look out for include *A.j.* 'Queen Charlotte' which has semi-double rich pink flowers with gold stamens and *A.j.* 'Alba' or the tall *A.j.* 'Honorine Jobert', both with large white flowers.
Height: 50–100 cm (18 in–3 ft 3 in). Plants per square metre: 5.

A garden on a very steep slope – down a flight of steps! This tiny basement garden shows how even the smallest space can be filled with plants in pots to create a colourful and welcoming entrance.

Elephant's ears *(Bergenia)*

These form large weed-suppressing clumps of very attractive, leathery, rounded evergreen leaves, some of which take on a bronze or red tint in winter. They also have spikes of white pink or red flowers in spring and summer. Good varieties include *B. cordifolia* 'Purpurea' which have large wavy round leaves turning a purplish-red in winter and magenta flowers on and off throughout the summer, *B.* 'Abendglut' with neat crinkle-edged leaves, good autumn colour and vivid rose-red flowers and *B.* 'Ballawley', the largest of all, with good autumn colour and rose-red flowers in spring and, occasionally, in autumn. Happy in sun or shade.
Height: 30 cm (15 in). Plants per square metre: 3.

Campanula

For ground cover at the front of a sunny border, *C. carpatica* with cup-shaped white or blue flowers is a good choice, as is lower growing, wider-spreading Fairy thimbles *C. cochleariifolia*. There are two very rampant varieties, both with impossible names, *C. poscharskyana* and *C. portenschlagiana*, which produce long trailing stems of starry blue flowers and which should only be planted where you have masses of space to fill. If they do exceed the space allotted, though, you can rip out the long stems very easily without damaging the plant.
Height (*C. carpatica*): 20 cm (8 in). Plants per square metre: 7.

Winter flowering heather *(Erica carnea)*

Although there is a lot of horticultural snobbery about heathers, they are excellent for low-maintenance gardens and not only form a weed-proof carpet but provide much-needed winter colour, from their flowers and from their foliage too. The winter-flowering kinds are happy in any type of soil and a sunny spot. Perhaps the secret in using them successfully is to plant them in bold drifts of seven or even nine of the same variety rather than lots of different ones. There are many excellent varieties, but the best include *E.c.* 'Ann Sparkes' with bright gold foliage and rich wine-red flowers, *E.c.* 'Myretoun Ruby' with dark green foliage and big ruby-red flowers and *E.c.* 'Springwood White' with bright green foliage and white flowers.
Height: to 25 cm (10 in). Plants per square metre: 5.

Spurge *(Euphorbia)*

Another good family with members to suit most situations. The best varieties for dry shade are the low-growing *E. cyparissias* which has lime-green flowers in early summer and *E. robbiae*, which is twice as tall! For a dry, sunny spot, try *E. myrsinites*, which produces low-growing grey stems with yellow flowers in early spring.
Height: from 15 cm (6 in) to 60 cm (2 ft). Plants per square metre: 3–5 (according to variety).

Crane's-bill (*Geranium*)

Another large family with members in all shapes and sizes with flowers ranging from white through blues, pinks and almost fluorescent magenta to a purple so deep it's almost black. Among the most widely available varieties are *G. endressii* 'Wargrave Pink', which produces its clear pink flowers from May to November, and the hybrid 'Johnson's Blue' which has clear blue cup-shaped flowers for many weeks in mid-summer. Not so widely available but well worth seeking out are the *G. macrorrhizums*, 'Album', 'Ingwersen's Variety' and 'Bevan's Variety', which to my mind are the best ground-cover geraniums of all, forming a weed-proof carpet of virtually evergreen, aromatic foliage which takes on a reddish tint in the autumn.

Also well worth trying are *G. renardii*, which has lovely scalloped, sage-green leaves and blush-white flowers veined with purple, *G. sanguineum* with a profusion of vivid magenta flowers all summer and *G. wallichianum* 'Buxton's Blue' which produces trailing stems of blue flowers with a white eye from mid-summer to autumn. It is ideal for growing among other plants whose flowering season has finished because it will trail over them making it look as though the host plant has begun to bloom again.

Height: 40 cm (16 in). Plants per square metre: 5.

Christmas rose (*Helleborus niger*) and Lenten rose (*Helleborus orientalis*)

These are ideal plants for a shady border. The Christmas rose (more often in flower during January than at Christmas) has leathery evergreen leaves and large, waxy white flowers with gold stamens that last for weeks. The Lenten rose which flowers in late winter has similar shaped flowers but in a whole range of colours from white and green through mauvy pinks to purple. It's a slightly larger plant than the Christmas rose and both of them are happy in limey soil.

Height: 30–45 cm (12–18 in). Plants per square metre: 5.

Coral flower (*Heuchera*)

Given a sunny spot and rich soil, this makes good weed-suppressing clumps of scalloped evergreen leaves and produces tall thin stems of tiny red or pink flowers. Two interesting varieties are *H.* 'Palace Purple' with mounds of bronzy, wine-coloured foliage and sprays of tiny white flowers (a good contrast with a silvery-leafed ground-cover plant like dead nettle (*Lamium*)) and *H. villosa* which has creamy green flowers some weeks after the rest of the family.

Height: 45 cm (18 in). Plants per square metre: 3.

Plantain lilies (*Hosta*)

These are outstanding foliage plants for a shady part of the garden and can form very large, weed-suppressing clumps. There are many different ones to choose from, some with small leaves like *H.* 'Ground Master' and some with huge leaves like *H. sieboldiana*

'Elegans'. There are gold-leafed varieties like *H. fortunei* 'Aurea', many shades of green, as well as blue and also variegated leaves like *H.* 'Thomas Hogg' whose elegant pointed leaves have creamy margins. They also flower, producing spikes of either mauve or white flowers in mid-summer.

The major snag with hostas is that slugs and snails love them almost as much as discerning gardeners do and can reduce a huge leaf to something resembling a punk colander overnight. While they are good ground cover, this means that their low-maintenance status is borderline. If you want to grow them you will need to use some kind of anti-slug precautions, either pellets or a liquid killer, or a mechanical barrier like cinders sprinkled around the plants. One city gardener found that spraying the leaves with a houseplant leaf shine deterred the slugs to a large extent but it did turn the beautiful blue-grey leaves of *H. sieboldiana* to a rather ordinary green.

Height (of foliage): 30–60 cm (1–2 ft). Plants per square metre: 5 or 3 according to size.

Dead nettle (*Lamium maculatum*)

This is a marvellous ground-cover plant for shade or for sun, spreading quickly and covering a large area with attractive variegated foliage. *L.m.* 'Beacon Silver', *L.m.* 'White Nancy' and *L.m.* 'Shell-Pink' all have silver variegated leaves and produce clear pink, ivory white and shell-pink flowers respectively in early to mid summer. After the flowers have faded you can trim the plant with shears to remove the dead flower heads and any upward-growing leafy shoots to keep it close to the ground.

Height: 20 cm (8 in). Plants per square metre: 5.

Creeping Jenny (*Lysimachia nummularia*)

This carpeter grows happily in part shade or in a sunny spot provided the soil is moist. It sends out long trailing evergreen growths which are smothered in yellow buttercup flowers in summer. The gold-leafed form *L.n.* 'Aurea' is not as vigorous.

Height: 2.5 cm (1 in). Plants per square metre: 3.

Omphalodes cappadocica

A very useful ground-cover plant for growing under acid-loving shrubs, and although its oval slightly crinkled leaves are not spectacular it produces sprays of the most vivid gentian-blue flowers, not unlike forget-me-nots but larger, for weeks on end in late spring and early summer.

Height: 20 cm (8 in). Plants per square metre: 5.

Knotweed or Bistort (*Polygonum* recently renamed *Persicaria*)

This is another large family, some of whose members, including the dreaded Japanese knotweed, are true garden thugs smothering everything in sight. Fortunately, others are better-behaved and make good weed-suppressing clumps. Good varieties to look out for

Pale pink and white roses and peonies complement perfectly the centrepiece
of this small front garden – the classic white urn.

include the low-growing *P. affine* 'Dimity', or 'Superba' whose pink, fluffy, poker flowers darken to a rusty red with age and whose fresh green foliage turns russet-brown in winter, staying on the plant until new growth appears in spring. If it does get over-ambitious, simply chop it back with a spade.
Height: 23 cm (9 in). Plants per square metre: 4.

Lungwort (*Pulmonaria*)
First class ground cover for moist shade with sprays of small pink, white or blue flowers in spring followed by clumps of weed-smothering, attractive spotted or silver-frosted leaves. Good varieties to look out for include *P. officinalis* 'Cambridge Blue' which has heart shaped, spotted leaves and masses of blue flowers opening from pink buds, giving it a bi-colour effect, *P. saccharata* 'Sissinghurst White', which has much larger leaves marbled with silver and large, pure white flowers and *P.s.* 'Highdown' which has rich blue flowers.
Height: 25 cm (10 in). Plants per square metre: 5.

London Pride (*Saxifraga* × *urbium*)

A good ground-cover plant for a shady spot where the soil isn't too dry, forming rosettes of leathery green leaves which throw up tall stems of tiny blush-white flowers in summer. **Height: 23 cm (9 in). Plants per square metre: 5.**

Stonecrop (*Sedum*)

Another good ground-cover family with its fair share of garden thugs. Biting stonecrop (*S. acre*) is sometimes advertised as the miracle ground-cover plant, and although it will certainly fill the space, it doesn't know where to stop, and once you've got it, you can never get rid of it. Choose better behaved relatives like *S. middendorfianum* whose leaves form bronze-green rosettes and which has starry yellow flowers in mid-summer and the silver-white *S. spathulifolium* 'Cape Blanco'. **Height: 8 cm (3 in). Plants per square metre: 8**

Lamb's lugs (*Stachys lanata* or *olympica*)

This plant has oval, woolly silver leaves which soon form a dense, weed-proof carpet. It has rather peculiar woolly flower spikes but 'Silver Carpet' doesn't flower. There is also a yellow form *S.* 'Primrose Heron'. **Height: 15 cm (6 in). Plants per square metre: 5**

Foamflower (*Tiarella cordifolia*)

A good evergreen plant for dappled shade with attractive lobed bright green leaves and sprays of small white flowers in early summer. Another relative *T. wherryi* has even more beautiful dark green leaves which develop a deep red blotch as they age and bears similar flowers later and for longer in the summer. **Height: 25 cm (10 in). Plants per square metre: 5.**

Viola labridorica 'Purpurea'

A superb ground-cover plant which seeds itself so freely when it's established that it could be a nuisance if it weren't so attractive! Just pull it out where you don't want it. It has small, roundish, heart-shaped green leaves flushed with purple, while its flowers, produced in spring, are small mauve violets whose colour is exactly right for the leaves. **Height: 10–15 cm (4–6 in). Plants per square metre: 7.**

Waldsteinia ternata

Another good evergreen carpeter for sun or shade with lovely glossy green leaves not unlike those of the strawberry and bright yellow strawberry flowers in the spring. **Height: 10 cm (4 in). Plants per square metre: 5.**

INDEX

157